Heart Healthy Diet Cookbook

1800 Days Healthy Recipes to Make a Long-Lasting Change in Your Heart Health with 30-Day Meal Plans

Zoe Storey

Copyright © 2021 by Zoe Storey- All rights reserved.

The content contained within this book may not be reproduced, duplicated, or transmitted without direct written permission from the author or the publisher. Under no circumstances will any blame or legal responsibility be held against the publisher, or author, for any damages, reparation, or monetary loss due to the information contained within this book, either directly or indirectly.

Legal Notice: This book is copyright protected. It is only for personal use. You cannot amend, distribute, sell, use, quote or paraphrase any part, or the content within this book, without the consent of the author or publisher.

Disclaimer Notice: Please note the information contained within this document is for educational and entertainment purposes only. All effort has been executed to present accurate, up to date, reliable, complete information. No warranties of any kind are declared or implied. Readers acknowledge that the author is not engaged in the rendering of legal, financial, medical, or professional advice. The content within this book has been derived from various sources. Please consult a licensed professional before attempting any techniques outlined in this book. By reading this document, the reader agrees that under no circumstances is the author responsible for any losses, direct or indirect, that are incurred as a result of the use of the information contained within this document, including, but not limited to, errors, omissions, or inaccuracies.

CONTENTS

INTRODUCTION 12

CHAPTER 1 HEART HEALTH MADE EASY 13

    What Is a Heart-Healthy Diet? 14

    Important Nutrients For Heart Health 15

    Nutrients That Are Bad For Heart Health 15

CHAPTER 2 BREAKFAST, BRUNCH AND BEVERAGES RECIPES 16

    Multigrain Waffles 16

    Southwest Breakfast Tofu 16

    Chocolate And Peanut Butter Smoothie 17

    Chocolate Power Smoothie 17

    Swiss Chard And Tzatziki Dip On Whole Wheat Toast 17

    Almond Butter And Blueberry Smoothie 17

    Almost-Instant Oatmeal 18

    Chocolate-Oatmeal Loaf 18

    Berry, Walnut, And Cinnamon Quinoa Bowl 18

    Artichoke, Basil, And Tomato Crustless Quiche 19

    California Scrambled Eggs And Veggies 19

    Strawberry Breakfast Sundae 19

    Kidney Bean Tortilla 20

    Apricot Granola With Fresh Fruit 20

    Sweet Potato And Turkey Hash 21

    Shakshuka 21

    Eggs In An Avocado 21

    Eggs Benedict With Low-Fat Béchamel Sauce 22

    Kefir Parfait With Chia Berry Jam 22

    Peaches And Cream Porridge 22

Lentil Asparagus Omelet 23

Peach-Cranberry Sunrise Muesli 23

Cashew Nut Shake 24

Southwest Sweet Potato Breakfast Hash 24

Baby Kale Breakfast Salad With Almond Butter Dressing 24

Tofu Shakshuka 25

Ginger-Mango Smoothie 25

Quinoa, Pistachio, And Blueberry Breakfast Bowl 25

Omelet With Zucchini, Mushrooms, And Peppers 26

Greek Yogurt Topped With Turmeric-Spiced Almonds And Pumpkin Seeds 26

Creamy Blueberry Quinoa Porridge 26

Strawberry Quinoa 27

Lemon Ricotta Pancake Bites 27

Apple Spiced Muffins 28

Almond Rice Breakfast Pudding 28

Breakfast Burrito 28

Raisin Cashew Oats 29

Spinach And Feta Frittata 29

Potato, Pepper, And Egg Breakfast Casserole 29

Soft-Boiled Egg Bites With Apricot Cheese Toasts 30

CHAPTER 3 POULTRY AND MEAT MAINS RECIPES 31

Southwest Steak Skillet 31

Grilled Garlic-Lime Chicken 31

Pineapple Chicken 32

Red Curry Beef Bowls 32

Apple Pork Stir-Fry 32

Rosemary Lemon Chicken With Vegetables 33

Blueberry, Pistachio, And Parsley Chicken 33

Ras El Hanout Lamb Stew 34

No-Fuss Turkey Breast	34
Balsamic Berry Chicken	34
Tuscan Turkey, White Beans, And Asparagus	35
Buffalo-Seasoned Chicken Wrap	35
Tahini And Turmeric Chicken Salad	36
Hawaiian Barbeque Chicken	36
Turkey Burgers	36
Turkey Cauliflower Burgers	37
Spicy Beef Roast	37
Asian Turkey Lettuce Wraps	38
Red Beans, Sausage, And Rice	38
Indian Butter Chicken	38
Braised Beef	39
Mushroom Bolognese	39
Chicken Lettuce Wrap With Peanut Dressing	40
Chicken Cacciatore	40
Salsa Verde Chicken	40
Beef And Vegetable Stew	41
Basil Pesto Chicken	41
Turkey And Mushroom Wild Rice Casserole	41
Parmesan Pork Chops	42
Spicy Turkey Wraps	42
Pan-Seared Pork Medallions With Pears	43
Lemon-Basil Chicken With Baby Bell Peppers	43
Alberta Steak Salad With Roasted Baby Potatoes	44
Oat Risotto With Mushrooms, Kale, And Chicken	44
Lamb Goulash	45
Tangy Italian Beef Sandwiches	45
Tomato Chicken Bake	45

Sliced Pork Loin For Sandwiches 46

Flank Steak And Hummus Salad 46

Garlic-Balsamic Beef Skewers 47

CHAPTER 4 FISH AND SEAFOOD MAINS RECIPES 48

Pine Nut Haddock 48

Citrus Tilapia 48

Fish Florentine 48

Lemon & Lime Tuna 49

Poached Fish In Tomato-Caper Sauce 49

Pistachio Flounder Fillets 50

Broiled Pesto Cod 50

Spicy Herring Pasta 50

Rainbow Trout Fillets With Parsley, Pecan, And Oranges 51

Pistachio-Crusted Halibut 51

Sofrito Cod Stew 52

Salmon Over Lentils 52

Mustard-Dill Salmon With Lemon And Asparagus 52

Mahi Mahi With Leeks, Ginger, And Baby Bok Choy 53

Pan-Seared Salmon With Chimichurri Sauce 53

Shrimp Paella 54

Tomato And Zucchini With Salmon And Farro 54

Mediterranean Mahi-Mahi 54

Lemon-Rosemary Salmon 55

Mussels With White Wine Sauce 55

Tuna, Cashew, And Couscous Salad 56

Creamy Tuna Salad 56

Pan-Seared Halibut With Chimichurri 56

Sheet Pan Tahini Cod With Broccoli 57

Cod Parcels With Mushrooms And Spinach 57

- Collard Green Halibut Wraps With Cilantro-Mint Sauce 57
- Shrimp Scampi 58
- Walnut-And-Herb–Crusted Fish 58
- Sardines Puttanesca 58
- Za'Atar Cod Fillets 59
- Electric Chickpeas And Shrimp 59
- Weeknight Fish Skillet 59
- Salmon Burgers With Dill 60
- Walnut-Crusted Halibut 60
- Salmon En Papillote With Sugar Snap Peas, Tomatoes, And Thyme 60
- Rosemary-Lemon Salmon 61
- Salmon Sage Bake 61
- "Home Late" Pantry Tilapia With Veggie Pasta 62
- Open-Faced Lemon Pepper Tuna Melt 62
- Fish And Chips With Homemade Tartar Sauce 63

CHAPTER 5 VEGETARIAN AND VEGAN MAINS RECIPES 64

- Lentil, Raisin, And Pecan Stuffed Acorn Squash 64
- Garbanzo Bean Curry 64
- Vegan Jambalaya 64
- Veggie Pizza With Cannellini Bean Crust 65
- Vegetarian Gyros 65
- Vegan Chickpea Chili 66
- Cauliflower, Tomato, And Green Pea Curry 66
- Pantry Beans And Rice 66
- Vegan Red Beans And Rice 67
- Tahini And Black Bean–Stuffed Sweet Potatoes 67
- Sweet Spot Lentil Salad 68
- Cannellini Bean Pizza 68
- Chickpea And Lentil Ratatouille 68

Chickpea And Spinach Saag 69

White Bean Soup With Orange And Celery 69

One-Skillet Southwest Quinoa And Vegetables 69

Spicy Bean And Rice–Stuffed Peppers 70

Feta And Black Bean–Stuffed Zucchini 70

Chickpea Sloppy Joes 71

Mushroom, Zucchini, And Chickpea Stuffed Tomatoes 71

White Bean Cabbage Casserole 72

Pile-It-High Veggie Sandwich 72

Mujaddara 72

Corn, Spinach, And Mushroom Soup 73

Tofu And Veggie "Ramen" With Soba Noodles 73

Butter Bean Penne 74

Spicy Spinach And Almond Stir-Fry 74

Chickpea Tikka Masala 75

Spicy Pear Tacos 75

Spaghetti Squash Stuffed With Kale, Artichokes, And Chickpeas 75

Chickpeas, Tomatoes, And Swiss Chard 76

Broccoli And Pasta With Peanut Sauce 76

Pocket Eggs With Sesame Sauce 77

Chickpea Gyros 77

Acorn Squash Stuffed With White Beans And Kale 77

Pasta E Fagioli 78

Lentil-Walnut Bolognese 78

Curried Soup With Cauliflower 79

Lentil And Fennel Salad 79

Vegetable Curry 80

CHAPTER 6 SALADS, SOUPS, AND SIDE DISHES RECIPES 81

Sautéed Kale With Blood Orange Dressing 81

Hearty Mashed Potatoes	81
Lime Wild Rice	81
Middle Eastern Bulgur Pilaf	82
Butternut Soup	82
Orange And Avocado Green Salad	82
Honey-Glazed Carrots	83
Mediterranean Cucumber, Tomato, And Kalamata Olive Salad	83
Rosemary Sweetato Mash	84
Spicy Bean Soup	84
Roasted Sweet Potatoes	84
Root Vegetable Stew	85
Roasted Lentil Snack Mix	85
Brussels Sprouts And Pancetta	85
Umami Mushrooms	86
Quinoa Spinach Power Salad	86
Baked Beet Salad	86
Cauliflower Steak With Arugula-Basil Pesto	87
Arugula Salad With Fennel	87
Quick Kale Caesar Salad	87
Vegetable Chips With Rosemary Salt	88
Lemon-Roasted Asparagus	88
Lemon Chicken Orzo Soup	88
Zucchini Noodles	89
Minestrone Soup	89
Brussel Sprouts Hummus	89
Granny Smith Salad	90
Sage-Roasted Baby Carrots	90
Roasted Peppers And Zucchini	90
Polenta Cakes	91

- Tempeh Taco Salad With Chile-Lime Glaze 91
- African Peanut Stew 91
- Warm Balsamic Beet Salad With Sunflower Seeds 92
- Garden Vegetable Stew With Toasted Cashews 92
- Moroccan Spiced Red Lentil And Millet Stew 93
- Roasted Eggplant With Tahini-Garlic Dressing 93
- Beet And Fennel Salad 93
- Roasted Summer Squash Farro Salad 94
- Simple Roasted Peppers 94
- Mixed Veg Crisps 95

CHAPTER 7 SAUCES, STAPLES, AND SWEET TREATS RECIPES 96

- Mushroom And Thyme Gravy 96
- Cinnamon-Vanilla Custard 96
- Vanilla Pear Crisp 96
- Sesame-Garlic Edamame 97
- Fruit-Infused Sparkling Water 97
- Cheesy Kale Chips 97
- Broiled Mango 98
- Zesty Carrot Tomato Sauce 98
- Italian Salad Dressing 98
- Rosemary-Garlic Cashews 99
- Hot Cocoa Cup 99
- Chile-Lime Glaze 99
- Basil-Walnut Pesto 99
- Cherry Chocolate Cake 100
- Turkey Stock 100
- Whole Wheat Seed Crackers 101
- Baked Apples With Cranberry-Walnut Filling 101
- Mushroom Gravy 101

Harvest Fruit Crisp 102

Barbeque Seasoning Rub Blend 102

Simple Veggie Broth 102

Spaghetti Sauce 103

Peanut Butter And Chocolate Black Bean Brownie 103

Raspberry-Lime Sorbet 103

Garlicky Kale Chips 104

Creamy Vegan Alfredo Sauce 104

Artichoke-Basil Hummus 104

Grano Dolce Light (Sweet Wheat) 105

Salt-Free Southwest Seasoning Mix 105

Chia Berry Jam 105

Spicy Guacamole 106

Maple Walnuts 106

Lemon-Tahini Dressing 106

Rosemary And White Bean Dip 106

Blueberry-Ricotta Swirl 107

Slow-Cooked Beans 107

Pumpkin Cakes 107

Mediterranean Seasoning Rub Blend 108

Date Brownies 108

Chocolate Mousse 108

30 DAY MEAL PLAN 109

RECIPES INDEX 111

Introduction

It can be overwhelming to tackle your unhealthy diet on your own. Information you search for online can be very confusing. Everyone seems to know the answer, but they all give conflicting advice. Eat eggs; don't eat eggs. Coconut oil is good for you; no it's not. Use butter in cooking; avoid butter altogether. And then your friends and family all have their say, as well. What do you believe?

The answers are found in sound scientific research. It may seem like even scientists are giving conflicting advice, but believe it or not, that is a good thing. If we had not made any progress in the world of health and nutrition research, we would still be miserable, eating egg white only omelets and dry toast.

Improved research methods and study designs mean that the scientific world can look at something they thought they knew, and say, "We are really sorry, but we got it wrong". Gone are the days when egg yolks were deemed off limits if you had high cholesterol. Butter is back on the table, and whole grain carbohydrates offer numerous health benefits.

The best diet for you is the one you can stick to. When you jump in the deep end, it can be difficult to hold your head above water. So many people take the all-or-nothing approach to changing their diet. They jump into a new eating pattern, full of enthusiasm and determination. But, you are going from a diet full of fatty, processed foods, to a diet that is completely foreign to you - one full of lean protein, whole grain carbohydrates and lots of vegetables - the wheels are going to come off. Much sooner than you might expect.

Eating for heart health is a long game. If you are prone to heart disease, it is something you are always going to have to manage. I had a conversation with my doctor who said that heart disease is a chronic disease - your management doesn't have to be perfect from day one. So, don't panic if you have just been diagnosed with high cholesterol or hypertension. Taking control of your diet is crucial, but it can be done slowly - one step at a time. That way you are more likely to make sustainable changes for long-lasting health.

You can change your health for the better, one meal at a time. Use our tasty, heart-healthy recipes to make new, lasting, healthy diet habits. You will see that your new way of eating is far from boring. In fact, you can use these recipes to cook for yourself, your family, and your friends.

Chapter 1 Heart Health Made Easy

Your heart-health journey begins here, and I'm thrilled to be the one you've chosen to guide you on your path to improved heart health. You can expect a ton of great information in the pages to come.

Not only will I introduce you to my nutrition philosophy as it relates to heart health, but also I will teach you the key groups of foods that will make all the difference going forward. You will leave this chapter with a much greater understanding of not only what to eat but also why certain foods are specifically beneficial to keep your heart working at its best. Although some of these messages may seem obvious to some of you, I promise to throw you a few curveballs while also addressing some of the more controversial topics in this corner of the nutrition world.

I don't want you to feel overwhelmed, though. I appreciate that this style of eating may be new to many of you, but I want you to know that this book will provide all the support and encouragement you need to succeed.

My goal is simply to make your transition into heart-healthier eating as seamless as possible, from our five-ingredient promise to listing the kitchen equipment you will need and everything in between.

Heart health made easy—what could be better? Let's get started.

What Is a Heart-Healthy Diet?

Let's start by defining some of the basic principles associated with the term "heart-healthy diet." This will help us arrive at a mutual understanding before we continue. I'd describe the term primarily as a style of eating that includes as many foods as possible known to directly reduce heart disease risk or reduce the risk factors associated with heart disease, such as high blood pressure, high blood cholesterol, or high blood triglyceride levels. My definition also allows room for foods that you truly enjoy so you can keep your heart healthy and happy in more ways than one.

Depending on personal preferences, this style of eating could look quite different from person to person, but here are some common themes across all heart-healthy diets:

High in vegetables (especially nonstarchy vegetables) and fruits

High in traditionally healthy fats such as fish, nuts, seeds, olives, avocado, etc.

High in plant-based protein sources such as legumes and soy, for those who enjoy them

High in aquatic protein sources such as fish and seafood

If you've been doing some investigating on your own in the nutrition world, you'll notice that most of these themes are common in many of the popularized heart-health approaches, such as the DASH diet, Mediterranean diet, vegan/vegetarianism, and the lesser-known but equally potent Portfolio diet.

Important Nutrients For Heart Health

The foods you eat to prevent and manage heart disease must contain notable quantities of the following nutrients, in order to keep your blood cholesterol and blood pressure under control:

Soluble fiber: Found in all legumes, such as beans, lentils, and chickpeas; fruits and vegetables; and grains, such as oats. Soluble fiber binds to cholesterol in the digestive tract, and prevents it from being absorbed into the bloodstream. Increasing your soluble fiber is an important dietary factor for controlling your cholesterol levels.

Unsaturated fats: Foods that are rich in unsaturated fatty acids, especially omega-3, have been linked to better cholesterol levels. Dark, oily fish, such as salmon, sardines, and mackerel, is the best source of omega-3 rich fats. But they are also found in nuts, seeds, avocado pears, and olive oil. Omega-3 fatty acids help to lower your total cholesterol level, reduce your LDL cholesterol, and increase your HDL cholesterol.

Potassium: An essential mineral for supporting healthy blood pressure, Potassium is found in fruit, vegetables, potatoes, whole grain carbohydrates, and avocado pears. Increasing your potassium intake is one of the many benefits of eating more plant-based foods.

Magnesium: The fourth most abundant mineral in the body, Magnesium is involved in more than six hundred chemical pathways in the body. It works closely with calcium to ensure the smooth contraction and relaxation of muscle tissues, including the heart. It helps to keep your heartbeat regular, and it also helps to lower your blood pressure. Dark green leafy vegetables, legumes, nuts, and seeds are good sources of magnesium

Calcium: Working closely with magnesium, calcium helps to regulate your heartbeat by ensuring the smooth contraction and relaxation of the muscle. It helps to maintain the health of your arteries, and so it is an important mineral for controlling your blood pressure. Food sources of calcium include low fat dairy products, dark green leafy vegetables, almonds, and fish with bones, such as canned salmon and sardines.

Nutrients That Are Bad For Heart Health

There are two components of the food we eat that can have a negative impact on your heart health. Scientific evidence can be confusing, but there is an overwhelming amount of evidence that links high levels of saturated fat, and/or sodium, to an increased risk for developing cardiovascular disease.

Saturated fat: Solid at room temperature, saturated fat is easy to identify. It is the fat on the side of your steak, or between the muscle fibers, the skin on chicken, full fat dairy products, cream, cheese, and coconut oil. Saturated fat provides the building blocks for cholesterol. It causes a rise in blood cholesterol levels, especially LDL (bad) cholesterol. Reducing your saturated fat intake can significantly reduce your cholesterol levels.

Sodium: The salt that is added to food during production, cooking, and at the table is the most significant source of sodium in our diet. There is a strong link between a high sodium intake and hypertension. You can improve your blood pressure by avoiding table salt, stock cubes, soup powder, salty snacks, and canned foods.

Chapter 2 Breakfast, Brunch And Beverages Recipes

Multigrain Waffles

Servings: 4
Cooking Time: 20 Min
Ingredients:
- ¾ cup whole-wheat flour
- ¼ cup ground flaxseed
- 3 tablespoons rolled oats
- 2 tablespoons unsalted sunflower seeds
- 1½ teaspoons baking powder
- 1½ teaspoons brown sugar
- ¼ teaspoon salt
- 1 cup 1% milk
- 2 tablespoons canola or sunflower oil
- 1 large egg

Directions:
1. Preheat a waffle iron.
2. Mix the flour, flaxseed, oats, sunflower seeds, baking powder, brown sugar, and salt in a large bowl. Add the milk, oil, and egg. Mix until just moistened.
3. Cover your waffle iron area with batter. Cook until golden and crisp (about 5 minutes for most waffle irons).
4. Serve immediately so the waffles are crisp and hot. If that's not possible, keep them warm directly on the rack in a 175°F oven.

Nutrition Info:
- Per Serving: Calories: 264 ; Fat: 15 g ;Cholesterol: 50 mg ;Sodium: 376 mg

Southwest Breakfast Tofu

Servings: 2
Cooking Time: 20 Min
Ingredients:
- 1 (1-pound) block medium-firm tofu
- ¼ red onion
- 1 red bell pepper
- 1 tablespoon extra-virgin olive oil
- 1 teaspoon reduced-sodium tamari
- 1 tablespoon nutritional yeast
- 2 teaspoons Salt-Free Southwest Seasoning Mix or Mrs. Dash, plus more if needed
- ⅛ to ¼ teaspoon salt (optional)
- 4 cups spinach
- 1 avocado, peeled, pitted, and diced (optional)

Directions:
1. Drain the tofu, then cut through its equator to make two flat blocks. Wrap them in a couple of layers of clean kitchen towel or paper towel for at least 5 minutes. (It doesn't need to be pressed completely dry as in some other recipes.)
2. Meanwhile, chop the onion and seed and thinly slice the red pepper.
3. Heat the oil in a large, nonstick skillet on medium-high heat. When hot, turn it down to medium and cook the onion and pepper until soft, 4 to 5 minutes, stirring occasionally.
4. While that's cooking, mix the tamari, nutritional yeast, Southwest seasoning, and ⅛ teaspoon of salt in a small bowl.
5. When the onion and pepper are ready, add the spinach to the pan. Turn the heat down to medium-low, and cover for 1 minute to steam. Transfer the veggies to a bowl, and cover to keep warm.
6. Add the tofu and the tamari mixture to the pan, and mix well to combine. Use a wooden spoon to crumble the tofu. Taste and add another ⅛ teaspoon of salt or more Southwest seasoning, if needed.
7. Return the vegetables to the pan, and mix just a little. Top with the avocado (if using).

Nutrition Info:
- Per Serving: Calories: 359 ; Fat: 26 g ;Cholesterol: 0 mg ;Sodium: 485 mg

Chocolate And Peanut Butter Smoothie

Servings: 1

Ingredients:
- 1 medium beet, peeled and quartered
- 1 tablespoon unsweetened cacao powder
- 2 teaspoons unsalted raw peanut butter
- ½ medium banana
- 3 ounces silken tofu
- 1 cup unsweetened almond milk

Directions:
1. Combine the beet, cacao powder, peanut butter, banana, tofu, and almond milk in a blender and blend for 1 to 2 minutes until well combined. Serve immediately.

Nutrition Info:
- Per Serving: Calories: 261 ; Fat: 11 g ;Cholesterol: 0 mg ;Sodium: 268 mg

Chocolate Power Smoothie

Servings: 2

Cooking Time: 10 Min

Ingredients:
- 1 medium frozen banana
- 1 cup baby spinach
- 1 cup frozen blueberries
- 2 tablespoons unsweetened cocoa powder
- 2 tablespoons natural peanut butter
- 1½ cups vanilla soy milk
- 1 tablespoon hemp seeds
- ¼ to ½ cup water (optional)

Directions:
1. If you don't have a very powerful blender, roughly chop the banana.
2. Combine the banana, spinach, blueberries, cocoa powder, peanut butter, soy milk, and hemp seeds in the blender, and purée very well. Add the water, a few tablespoons at a time, if you prefer a thinner consistency.

Nutrition Info:
- Per Serving: Calories: 285 ; Fat: 13g ;Cholesterol: 0 mg ;Sodium: 180 mg

Swiss Chard And Tzatziki Dip On Whole Wheat Toast

Servings: 2

Cooking Time: 10 Minutes

Ingredients:
- 1 teaspoon avocado oil
- 1 small onion, chopped
- 2 garlic cloves, thinly sliced
- 1 bunch Swiss chard, stems diced and leaves chopped, divided
- 2 slices low-sodium whole wheat bread
- 1 cup Tzatziki Dip

Directions:
1. In a medium pot, heat the oil over medium-low heat and add the onion, garlic, and Swiss chard stems. Heat for 5 minutes, until the onions become translucent and the chard stalks bleed red into the dish.
2. Add the chard leaves and cover for 5 minutes, until the leaves are wilted and the dish is fragrant.
3. Meanwhile, toast the bread until crisp. Place it on a serving plate and top each slice of bread with 1 cup of cooked Swiss chard and ½ cup of the dip.

Nutrition Info:
- Per Serving: Calories: 214 ; Fat: 4 g ;Cholesterol: 5 mg ;Sodium: 111 mg

Almond Butter And Blueberry Smoothie

Servings: 2

Ingredients:
- 2 cups frozen blueberries
- 1¾ cups unsweetened almond milk
- 1 cup frozen spinach
- ¼ cup almond butter
- ½ cup ice

Directions:

1. In a blender, combine the blueberries, almond milk, spinach, and almond butter. Process until smooth.
2. Add the ice, and blend again until smooth.

Nutrition Info:

- Per Serving: Calories:324 ; Fat: 22g ;Cholesterol: 0mg ;Sodium: 186mg

Almost-Instant Oatmeal

Servings: 2
Cooking Time: 10 Min
Ingredients:

- 2 cups vanilla soy milk, plus more if needed
- ¾ cup oat bran
- 2 tablespoons natural peanut butter
- 2 teaspoons pure maple syrup
- ¼ teaspoon ground cinnamon
- 1 banana, sliced, divided
- 1 tablespoon hemp seeds, divided

Directions:

1. Heat the soy milk in a large pot over high heat. Add the oat bran, peanut butter, maple syrup, and cinnamon, stirring as you go. When it starts to boil, turn the heat down to medium-low.
2. Cook for 2 minutes, stirring occasionally. Add more milk or water if you prefer a thinner consistency.
3. Divided the oatmeal between two bowls. Top each with half of the sliced banana and hemp seeds.

Nutrition Info:

- Per Serving: Calories: 354 ; Fat: 15 g ;Cholesterol: 0 mg ;Sodium: 123 mg

Chocolate-Oatmeal Loaf

Servings: 6
Cooking Time: 20 Minutes
Ingredients:

- Nonstick avocado oil cooking spray
- 2 tablespoons ground flaxseed
- 5 tablespoons unsweetened organic soymilk
- 1¼ cups rolled oats
- 1 teaspoon baking powder
- 2 tablespoons unsweetened cacao powder
- 1 teaspoon cinnamon
- 1 tablespoon pure maple syrup
- 1 banana, mashed
- 2 tablespoons unsalted raw almond butter

Directions:

1. Preheat the oven to 400°F. Spray a standard (8½-by-4½-by-2½-inch) loaf pan with cooking spray or grease it with 1 teaspoon of oil spread equally on the sides. Place the pan in the oven.
2. In a small mixing bowl, mix the flaxseed and soymilk and let the mixture sit for 5 minutes, until it congeals.
3. In a large mixing bowl, combine the oats, baking powder, cacao powder, and cinnamon and mix well. In a small mixing bowl, combine the maple syrup, banana, almond butter, and flaxseed mixture and mix well. Add the dry ingredients into the wet ingredients until well combined.
4. Carefully take the loaf pan out of the oven and pour the mixture into it. Bake for 20 minutes, or until a fork inserted into the middle of the loaf comes out clean. This loaf is best served warm. Store in the refrigerator covered for up to 1 week. To rewarm, heat in the microwave in 15-second increments until warm.

Nutrition Info:

- Per Serving: Calories:152 ; Fat: 6 g ;Cholesterol: 0 mg ;Sodium: 89 mg

Berry, Walnut, And Cinnamon Quinoa Bowl

Servings: 2
Cooking Time: 15 Minutes
Ingredients:

- ½ cup quinoa
- 1 cup unsweetened almond milk
- 1 teaspoon cinnamon, plus more for coating
- 10 raw walnuts
- 1 cup strawberries, sliced

Directions:

1. Preheat the oven to 425°F and line a baking sheet with parchment paper. In a medium pot, bring the quinoa, almond milk, and cinnamon to a boil.

2. Lower the heat to a simmer and cover for 12 minutes, or until the almond milk has been absorbed.
3. Put the walnuts and a dash of cinnamon onto the prepared baking sheet and bake for 5 minutes until lightly golden.
4. In a serving bowl, combine the quinoa and walnuts, and top with the strawberries. (When storing, put the quinoa only in the refrigerator for up to 1 week. Add the walnuts and strawberries when ready to eat.)

Nutrition Info:
- Per Serving: Calories: 268 ; Fat: 11 g ;Cholesterol: 0 mg ;Sodium: 88 mg

Artichoke, Basil, And Tomato Crustless Quiche

Servings: 4
Cooking Time: 20 Minutes
Ingredients:
- 2 cups artichoke hearts, finely chopped
- ⅓ cup chopped fresh basil
- 1 cup cherry tomatoes, halved
- ¾ teaspoon freshly ground black pepper
- ¼ cup part-skim ricotta cheese
- 4 whole eggs
- 8 egg whites
- Avocado oil spray

Directions:
1. Preheat the oven to 400°F.
2. In a large mixing bowl, mix the artichoke hearts, basil, tomatoes, pepper, ricotta cheese, whole eggs, and egg whites, and combine well.
3. Spray a large oven-safe dish with cooking spray (or evenly grease it with 1 teaspoon of avocado oil). Pour the mixture into a cast-iron skillet or oven-safe pan and bake in the oven for 15 minutes at 400°F, then increase the heat to 425°F for an additional 5 minutes, until the eggs are baked through and the edges are slightly browned. After cooled for at least 10 minutes, divide into 4 or 8 even pieces and serve, or store in the refrigerator for 5 to 7 days.

Nutrition Info:
- Per Serving: Calories: 160 ; Fat: 6 g ;Cholesterol: 169 mg ;Sodium: 250 mg

California Scrambled Eggs And Veggies

Servings: 2
Cooking Time: 15 Min
Ingredients:
- 4 large eggs
- Pinch salt
- Freshly ground black pepper
- 2 teaspoons Better Butter or 1 teaspoon extra-virgin olive oil plus 1 teaspoon unsalted butter
- Handful of arugula leaves, chopped
- 8 cherry tomatoes, halved
- ¼ cup chopped Simple Roasted Peppers or jarred roasted red peppers (optional)
- 1 avocado, peeled, pitted, and diced

Directions:
1. Crack the eggs into a large bowl. Season with salt and pepper, and whisk well.
2. In a large, nonstick skillet, melt the Better Butter over medium-low heat. When it starts to froth, add the arugula and sauté for a minute. Slide the arugula out of the pan and onto a plate.
3. Pour the eggs into the pan, and stir occasionally to scramble. When the eggs are almost done, sprinkle in the tomatoes, wilted arugula, and red pepper (if using). Don't stir. Put the lid on the pan, and cook for 1 more minute.
4. Top with the avocado.

Nutrition Info:
- Per Serving: Calories: 315 ; Fat: 24 g ;Cholesterol: 377 mg ;Sodium: 393 mg

Strawberry Breakfast Sundae

Servings: 2
Cooking Time: 5 Min
Ingredients:
- 1 cup plain 2% Greek yogurt, divided
- 1 banana, sliced, divided
- ½ cup Omega-3 Skillet Granola or store-bought low-sugar granola, divided
- ¼ cup slivered almonds, divided
- 1 cup strawberries, divided

Directions:
1. Divide the yogurt between two bowls.
2. Top each with half of the sliced banana, granola, almonds, and strawberries.

Nutrition Info:
- Per Serving: Calories: 415 ; Fat: 22 g ;Cholesterol: 18 mg ;Sodium: 91 mg

Kidney Bean Tortilla

Servings: 2
Cooking Time: 5 Min
Ingredients:
- 1 cup canned kidney beans, drained and rinsed
- ½ ripe avocado, peeled, pitted, and diced
- ½ medium mango, diced
- 1 lime, juiced
- ¼ cup parsley, chopped
- 1 tbsp apple cider vinegar
- 1 large egg, poached
- 2 whole-wheat tortillas

Directions:
1. In a medium sized mixing bowl, add the kidney beans, diced avocado, diced mango, lime juice, and chopped parsley, mix to combine.
2. Fill a medium sized stockpot with water halfway and bring to a boil and add the apple cider vinegar.
3. Crack the large egg into a small sized mixing bowl. Reduce the heat to a simmer. Mix the water with a spoon to create a whirlpool. Gently drop the egg inside, and cook for 3 minutes, until the egg white has set. Remove carefully with a slotted spoon and place on a paper towel to drain.
4. Spread the kidney bean mixture on a whole-wheat tortilla, place the poached egg on top and serve.

Nutrition Info:
- Per Serving: Calories: 294 ; Fat: 7 g ;Cholesterol: 0 mg ;Sodium: 130 mg

Apricot Granola With Fresh Fruit

Cooking Time: 5 Minutes
Ingredients:
- ¼ cup gluten-free rolled oats
- 2 tablespoons almonds
- 2 tablespoons walnuts
- 2 tablespoons ground flaxseed
- ¾ tablespoon olive oil
- 1 tablespoon maple syrup
- Pinch ground cinnamon
- ¼ cup chopped dried apricots
- 1 mango, peeled and chopped
- ¾ cup fresh strawberries
- ½ cup fresh blueberries
- Nonfat dairy milk or plant-based milk, for topping

Directions:
1. Add the oats, almonds, walnuts, and flaxseed to a small pan over medium heat.
2. Stir until the oats and nuts are warm and starting to brown, 3 to 4 minutes.
3. Pour the olive oil into the pan and stir until mixed through.
4. Pour the maple syrup into the pan and stir until mixed through.
5. Add the cinnamon and stir, then add the dried apricots and mix until combined.
6. Take off the heat and let it cool.
7. Peel and chop the mango, wash and slice the strawberries, and wash the blueberries.
8. Portion the granola into two serving bowls and top with the fresh fruit and milk.
9. Enjoy immediately.

Nutrition Info:
- Per Serving: Calories: 378 ; Fat: 17 g ;Cholesterol: 0 mg ;Sodium: 6 mg

Sweet Potato And Turkey Hash

Servings: 4
Cooking Time: 25 Minutes
Ingredients:
- 2½ tablespoons extra-virgin olive oil, divided
- 12 ounces ground turkey
- ½ teaspoon ground fennel seed
- Salt
- Freshly ground black pepper
- 1 pound sweet potato, diced
- 4 large eggs
- ¼ cup chopped fresh parsley

Directions:
1. In a large skillet, heat 1 tablespoon of oil over medium-high heat.
2. Add the turkey, and cook, stirring regularly, for 4 to 6 minutes, or until cooked through.
3. Stir in the ground fennel. Season with salt and pepper. Transfer to a plate.
4. In the same skillet, heat 1 tablespoon of oil over medium-high heat.
5. Add the sweet potato, and cook for 10 to 12 minutes, or until cooked through and browned.
6. Return the turkey to the skillet, mix well, then divide the hash among 4 plates.
7. Pour the remaining ½ tablespoon of oil into the skillet, and heat over medium-high heat.
8. Crack the eggs into the skillet, and cook for 3 minutes, or until set.
9. Flip the eggs, and cook for 30 seconds to 1 minute, or to your desired doneness. Remove from the heat.
10. Top each portion with an egg, and garnish with the parsley.

Nutrition Info:
- Per Serving: Calories: 374 ; Fat: 20 g ;Cholesterol: 0mg ;Sodium: 233 mg

Shakshuka

Servings: 4
Cooking Time: 25 Minutes
Ingredients:
- 1 tablespoon extra-virgin olive oil
- 1 red bell pepper, chopped
- 1 (28-ounce) can low-sodium diced tomatoes
- 1 teaspoon ground cumin
- Salt
- Freshly ground black pepper
- 4 large eggs
- ¼ cup chopped fresh parsley

Directions:
1. In a large skillet, heat the oil over medium-high heat.
2. Add the bell pepper, and cook for 4 to 6 minutes, or until softened.
3. Add the tomatoes with their juices and the cumin. Bring to a simmer. Cook for 10 minutes, or until the flavors meld and the sauce thickens. Season with salt and pepper.
4. Using a large spoon, make 4 depressions in the tomato mixture. Crack an egg into each depression. Cover the skillet, and cook for 5 to 7 minutes, depending on your desired doneness. Remove from the heat.
5. Serve the shakshuka topped with the parsley.

Nutrition Info:
- Per Serving: Calories: 146 ; Fat: 9 g ;Cholesterol: 0mg ;Sodium: 102 mg

Eggs In An Avocado

Cooking Time: 5 Minutes
Ingredients:
- 1 large avocado, halved, pitted, and peeled
- Salt
- Freshly ground black pepper
- 1 tablespoon olive oil, divided
- 2 large eggs
- 3 or 4 tablespoons water
- ½ cup halved cherry tomatoes
- ¼ cup chopped fresh chives

Directions:
1. Lay the avocado halves on a clean work surface, hollow-side up. Gently press the avocado down to slightly flatten the bottom so it will sit without tipping. (Keep the hollow part of the avocado intact to crack the eggs into later.) Season with salt and pepper.

2. Heat ½ tablespoon of olive oil in a high-sided skillet over medium-high heat. Add the avocado halves, hollow-side up. Allow the avocados to sear for 1 minute. Crack an egg into each hollow. Season the eggs with salt and pepper. Pour 3 or 4 tablespoons of water into the bottom of the pan and cover the pan with a lid. Bring the water to a simmer and let the eggs steam for 3 to 5 minutes, or until the egg whites have set and the yolks are firm (or set to your liking).
3. Meanwhile, in a medium bowl, mix together the tomatoes, chives, and remaining ½ tablespoon of olive oil. Season with salt and pepper.
4. Remove the egg-stuffed avocados to two serving plates. Top with the tomato and chive mixture and serve

Nutrition Info:
- Per Serving: Calories: 346 ; Fat:32 g ;Cholesterol: 186 mg ;Sodium: 156 mg

complete, quick release the pressure. Remove the lid and lift out the egg mold and the trivet. Dump out the water, dry the inner pot, and return it to the Instant Pot.
4. Pour the milk and egg yolk into the inner pot. Select Sauté and cook, whisking continuously, for 30 seconds, until thoroughly combined. Whisk in the flour, garlic powder, and Parmesan; keep whisking until the liquid comes to a boil and starts to thicken. Press Cancel and stir in the lemon juice. Season with black pepper (if using).
5. Divide the English muffin halves among four plates. Top each muffin half with ½ cup of spinach, 1 poached egg, and ¼ cup of béchamel sauce and serve.

Nutrition Info:
- Per Serving: Calories: 187 ; Fat: 7 g ;Cholesterol: 207 mg ;Sodium: 237 mg

Eggs Benedict With Low-Fat Béchamel Sauce

Servings: 4
Cooking Time: 2 Minutes
Ingredients:
- 1½ cups water
- Nonstick cooking spray
- 4 medium eggs
- ¾ cup low-fat milk
- 1 medium egg yolk
- 1 tablespoon all-purpose flour
- ¼ teaspoon garlic powder
- 1 tablespoon grated Parmesan cheese
- Juice of 1 lemon
- Freshly ground black pepper (optional)
- 2 whole wheat English muffins, split and toasted
- 2 cups baby spinach

Directions:
1. Pour 1½ cups of water into the Instant Pot and set the trivet in the center.
2. Coat a 7-cup silicone egg mold with nonstick spray. Crack each egg into a well of the egg mold. Cover the mold with its lid or aluminum foil and set it on the trivet.
3. Lock the lid into place. Select Pressure Cook and cook on high pressure for 2 minutes. When the cooking is

Kefir Parfait With Chia Berry Jam

Servings: 2
Ingredients:
- 12 ounces low-fat kefir
- 4 tablespoons Chia Berry Jam

Directions:
1. Into each of two serving bowls, place half of the kefir and 2 tablespoons of chia jam and dig in!

Nutrition Info:
- Per Serving: Calories:113 ; Fat:3 g ;Cholesterol: 9 mg ;Sodium: 71 mg

Peaches And Cream Porridge

Servings: 4
Cooking Time: 12 Minutes
Ingredients:
- 3 cups low-fat milk, divided
- 8 small dates, pitted and chopped
- 1 tablespoon shelled pistachios
- 6 tablespoons farina
- 1 cup canned unsweetened sliced peaches, drained
- Ground cinnamon (optional)

Directions:
1. Select Sauté. In the inner pot, combine 2 cups of milk, the dates, and the pistachios and stir together. Cook until the mixture comes to a boil, about 5 minutes, then, while whisking continuously, slowly add the farina, 1 tablespoon at a time, and whisk for about 1 minute, until it starts to thicken. Press Cancel.
2. Add the peaches and cover the pot (without sealing the lid). Let stand for 1 to 2 minutes, until the porridge is thick and creamy.
3. Divide the porridge among four bowls and top each with ¼ cup of the remaining milk and a pinch of cinnamon, if desired.

Nutrition Info:
- Per Serving: Calories: 214 ; Fat: 1.3 g ;Cholesterol: 9 mg ;Sodium: 126 mg

Lentil Asparagus Omelet

Cooking Time: 10 Minutes
Ingredients:
- 4 eggs, whisked
- 1 tablespoon dried thyme
- ¼ cup chopped onion
- 1 cup chopped asparagus (about ½ pound asparagus)
- ½ cup canned lentils, drained and rinsed
- ½ cup chopped grape tomatoes, for garnish
- 8 avocado slices, for garnish (optional)

Directions:
1. In a medium bowl, whisk together the eggs and thyme. Set them aside.
2. Heat a small nonstick skillet over medium heat. Add the onion and asparagus and cook for 2 to 3 minutes. Add the lentils and cook for an additional 2 minutes until heated through. Decrease the heat to low to keep warm.
3. Heat a medium nonstick skillet over medium heat. Whisk the eggs once more, then add half of the eggs to the frying pan and cook for 2 to 3 minutes.
4. Spread half of the asparagus-lentil mixture on one half of the eggs. Cook for 1 to 2 minutes more, then fold the egg over the filling and cook for another 1 to 2 minutes. Remove from the pan and place on a serving plate.
5. Repeat with the remaining ingredients to make the second omelet.
6. Garnish with the chopped tomatoes and avocado slices (if using) and serve immediately.

Nutrition Info:
- Per Serving: Calories: 242 ; Fat: 9 g ;Cholesterol: 327mg ;Sodium: 129mg

Peach-Cranberry Sunrise Muesli

Servings: 1
Cooking Time: 15 Min
Ingredients:
- ⅓ cup vanilla soy milk
- 3 tablespoons rolled oats
- 1 tablespoon chia seeds
- 1 tablespoon buckwheat (optional, see tip)
- 1 peach
- 1 tablespoon dried cranberries
- 1 tablespoon sunflower seeds

Directions:
1. Mix the soy milk, oats, chia seeds, and buckwheat (if using) in a large bowl. Soak for at least 10 minutes (and as long as overnight).
2. Meanwhile, cut the peach into bite-size pieces.
3. When the oats have softened up, sprinkle with the cranberries, sunflower seeds, and peach chunks.

Nutrition Info:
- Per Serving: Calories: 361 ; Fat: 11 g ;Cholesterol: 0 mg ;Sodium: 42 mg

Cashew Nut Shake

Servings: 1
Cooking Time: 10 Min
Ingredients:
- 2 cups spinach
- 1 tbsp unsweetened cacao powder
- 2 tsp unsalted cashew butter
- ½ medium banana
- 3 oz firm tofu
- 1 cup unsweetened cashew milk
- ¼ cup unsalted cashew nuts

Directions:
1. In a blender, add the spinach, unsweetened cacao powder, cashew butter, banana, firm tofu, cashew milk and unsalted cashew nuts, blend on high speed for 1 to 2 minutes until smooth and no lumps remain.
2. Serve immediately.

Nutrition Info:
- Per Serving: Calories: 261 ; Fat: 11 g ;Cholesterol: 0 mg ;Sodium: 268 mg

Southwest Sweet Potato Breakfast Hash

Cooking Time: 25 Minutes
Ingredients:
- For the sweet potato hash
- 2 teaspoons olive oil
- 1 garlic clove, minced
- 1 cup diced yellow onion
- 2 cups peeled and cubed sweet potatoes
- 1 cup canned black beans, drained and rinsed
- ½ teaspoon paprika
- ½ teaspoon ground cumin
- Pinch salt
- ¼ cup chopped fresh cilantro
- For the guacamole
- ½ avocado, peeled, seeded, and mashed
- Juice of ½ lime
- Salt
- For the pico de gallo
- ½ cup diced grape tomatoes
- ¼ cup finely diced white onion
- ¼ cup chopped fresh cilantro
- Salt

Directions:
1. TO MAKE THE SWEET POTATO HASH
2. Heat the olive oil in a large skillet over medium heat. Add the garlic, onion, sweet potatoes, black beans, paprika, cumin, and salt. Cook for 20 to 25 minutes, stirring every few minutes until the potatoes become tender and slightly caramelized. Remove from the heat and stir in the fresh cilantro.
3. TO MAKE THE GUACAMOLE
4. In a small bowl, stir together the mashed avocado and lime juice. Season with salt and set it aside.
5. TO MAKE THE PICO DE GALLO
6. In a small bowl, stir together the tomatoes, onion, and cilantro. Season with salt and set it aside.
7. TO ASSEMBLE
8. Spoon the sweet potato hash onto two plates, and top with the pico de gallo and guacamole. Serve immediately.

Nutrition Info:
- Per Serving: Calories: 528 ; Fat: 16 g ;Cholesterol: 0 mg ;Sodium: 260 mg

Baby Kale Breakfast Salad With Almond Butter Dressing

Cooking Time: 10 Minutes
Ingredients:
- For the salad
- 4 cups baby kale
- 1 (7.5 ounce) jar artichoke hearts packed in water, drained
- 1 (15-ounce) can chickpeas, drained and rinsed
- 1 cup grape tomatoes, halved
- 2 tablespoons hemp seeds
- For the dressing
- ¼ cup almond butter
- Juice of 1 lemon
- 1 tablespoon low-sodium soy sauce
- 1 tablespoon minced garlic
- 1 tablespoon minced ginger

- 2 tablespoons water, plus more as needed

Directions:
1. TO MAKE THE SALAD
2. Wash and dry the baby kale. Set it aside.
3. In a medium bowl, combine the artichoke hearts, chickpeas, tomatoes, and hemp seeds.
4. TO MAKE THE DRESSING
5. In a small bowl, whisk together all the dressing ingredients, adding additional water as needed to get to the desired consistency.
6. Add the dressing to the artichoke mix and combine until evenly coated.
7. Divide the baby kale between two serving plates. Top with half of the artichoke mixture and serve immediately.

Nutrition Info:
- Per Serving: Calories: 500 ; Fat: 11 g ;Cholesterol: 0 mg ;Sodium: 1,056 mg

Tofu Shakshuka

Servings: 4
Cooking Time: 15 Minutes
Ingredients:
- 2 teaspoons avocado oil
- 1 large onion, diced
- 1 large red bell pepper, diced
- 2 large tomatoes, diced
- 3 tablespoons double-concentrated tomato paste
- ½ cup water
- 1 (14-ounce) package firm tofu, cut into 1-inch-thick square pieces
- 4 heaping tablespoons chopped fresh basil
- 2 teaspoons Mediterranean Seasoning Rub Blend

Directions:
1. In a large pot, heat the oil over medium heat. Add the onion, bell pepper, and tomatoes and cook for about 2 minutes, until the onions are translucent. Add the tomato paste and water to the pot, stir, and cover. Cook for 5 minutes, until the peppers are fork-tender and the tomatoes are soft.
2. Add the tofu, basil, and spice blend and combine well with other ingredients. Cook, covered, for another 5 to 10 minutes, until fragrant, stirring occasionally. Divide among four plates and serve, or store in an airtight container in the refrigerator for up to 5 days.

Nutrition Info:
- Per Serving: Calories: 227 ; Fat: 12 g ;Cholesterol: 0 mg ;Sodium: 87 mg

Ginger-Mango Smoothie

Servings: 1
Ingredients:
- ½ cup frozen mango
- 1 cup spinach
- ½ cup low-fat, plain Greek yogurt
- ½ inch ginger, peeled
- 3 tablespoons water, as needed to thin

Directions:
1. Combine the mango, spinach, yogurt, and ginger in a blender. Blend to your desired thickness, adding water as necessary. Serve immediately.

Nutrition Info:
- Per Serving: Calories: 148 ; Fat: 3 g ;Cholesterol: 10 mg ;Sodium: 67 mg

Quinoa, Pistachio, And Blueberry Breakfast Bowl

Servings: 4
Cooking Time: 20 Minutes
Ingredients:
- 1¾ cups water
- 1 cup quinoa
- Pinch salt
- 2 cups blueberries
- ½ cup shelled pistachios
- 1 cup unsweetened almond milk
- 4 teaspoons honey

Directions:

1. In a saucepan, combine the water, quinoa, and salt. Bring to a boil.
2. Reduce the heat to a simmer. Cover the saucepan, and cook for 15 minutes, or until the water has been absorbed. Remove from the heat. Let sit for 5 minutes.
3. Evenly distribute the quinoa (about ¾ cup each), blueberries, and pistachios among 4 bowls.
4. Pour the almond milk on top, and drizzle with the honey.

Nutrition Info:
- Per Serving: Calories: 313 ; Fat: 10 g ;Cholesterol: 0mg ;Sodium: 33 mg

Omelet With Zucchini, Mushrooms, And Peppers

Servings: 2
Cooking Time: 10 Minutes
Ingredients:
- 1 tablespoon extra-virgin olive oil
- ½ small zucchini, chopped
- 1 cup sliced mushrooms
- ½ cup chopped cored bell pepper
- 1 teaspoon fresh thyme leaves
- Salt
- Freshly ground black pepper
- 4 large eggs

Directions:
1. In a large nonstick skillet, heat the oil over medium heat.
2. Add the zucchini, mushrooms, and bell pepper. Sauté for 5 to 6 minutes, or until softened and lightly browned.
3. Stir in the thyme. Season lightly with salt and pepper. Transfer to a plate.
4. In a small bowl, whisk the eggs. Season lightly with salt and pepper.
5. Pour the eggs into the same skillet, and cook for 2 to 3 minutes over medium heat, or until set.
6. Place the vegetables on one side of the eggs, and fold the other side over them. Cook for about 1 minute, then using a spatula, flip to the other side to heat through. Remove from the heat. Divide the omelet evenly onto 2 plates, and serve.

Nutrition Info:
- Per Serving: Calories: 223 ; Fat:17 g ;Cholesterol: 0mg ;Sodium: 225 mg

Greek Yogurt Topped With Turmeric-Spiced Almonds And Pumpkin Seeds

Servings: 2
Cooking Time: 10 Minutes
Ingredients:
- ¼ teaspoon ground turmeric
- ¼ teaspoon cinnamon powder
- ⅛ teaspoon freshly ground black pepper
- ¼ cup raw almonds, sliced
- ¼ cup raw pumpkin seeds
- 2 cups fat-free or low-fat plain Greek yogurt

Directions:
1. Preheat the oven to 425°F. Line a baking sheet with parchment paper.
2. On the baking sheet pan, mix the turmeric, cinnamon, and black pepper with the almonds and pumpkin seeds. Spread them out once thoroughly mixed, so they do not overlap.
3. Bake for 5 to 8 minutes, until golden brown and fragrant.
4. To serve, fill each serving bowl with 1 cup of yogurt and top with the nut and seed mixture. Store nuts in an airtight container in the refrigerator for up to 5 days.

Nutrition Info:
- Per Serving: Calories: 310 ; Fat: 15 g ;Cholesterol: 12 mg ;Sodium: 91 mg

Creamy Blueberry Quinoa Porridge

Servings: 2
Cooking Time: 15 Min
Ingredients:
- ½ cup uncooked quinoa
- 1 cup 1% milk
- ½ cup water
- 1 cup Blueberry-Chia Jam, divided
- 2 tablespoons oat bran
- ⅓ cup chopped walnuts, divided
- 2 teaspoons pure maple syrup (optional), divided

Directions:
1. Heat the quinoa, milk, and water in a medium pot over medium-high heat. When it starts to simmer, turn the heat to low, cover, and cook for 13 minutes (set a timer).
2. Meanwhile, reheat the chia jam in a small pot or in the microwave.
3. When the timer rings, add the oat bran to the quinoa, cover, and simmer for another 5 minutes.
4. Divide the porridge between two bowls. Top each with half of the chia jam, walnuts, and a drizzle of maple syrup (if using).

Nutrition Info:
- Per Serving: Calories: 423 ; Fat: 18 g ;Cholesterol: 6 mg ;Sodium: 58 mg

Strawberry Quinoa

Servings: 4
Cooking Time: 20 Min
Ingredients:
- 1¾ cups water
- 1 cup quinoa
- Pinch Himalayan pink salt
- 2 cups strawberries, sliced
- ½ cup unsalted cashew nuts, chopped
- 1 cup unsweetened cashew milk
- 4 tsp honey

Directions:
1. In a medium sized stockpot, add the water, quinoa, and Himalayan pink salt. Mix to combine and allow to boil.
2. Reduce the heat to low, cover, and cook for 15 minutes until the water has been absorbed. Remove from the heat and allow to stand for 5 minutes.
3. Divide ¾ cup of quinoa, sliced strawberries, chopped cashews into 4 serving bowls.
4. Add in the cashew milk and drizzle with honey. Serve warm or cold.

Nutrition Info:
- Per Serving: Calories: 313 ; Fat: 10 g ;Cholesterol: 0mg ;Sodium: 33 mg

Lemon Ricotta Pancake Bites

Servings: 4
Cooking Time: 7 Minutes
Ingredients:
- 2 medium eggs, separated
- ¾ cup low-fat milk
- 1 teaspoon olive oil or avocado oil
- 1 cup all-purpose flour
- 1 teaspoon baking powder
- 1½ cups water
- Nonstick cooking spray
- ¾ cup low-fat ricotta cheese, divided
- Juice of 1 lemon
- 2 tablespoons maple syrup
- 2 cups thawed frozen wild blueberries

Directions:
1. In a medium bowl, whip the egg whites with a hand mixer until soft peaks form.
2. In a separate medium bowl, whisk together the egg yolks, milk, and oil. Stir in the flour and baking powder until well combined. Gently fold in the whipped egg whites.
3. Pour 1½ cups of water into the Instant Pot and set the trivet in the center.
4. Coat a 7-cup silicone egg mold with nonstick spray. Pour the batter into the egg mold, filling each well about halfway. Add a small dollop (about 1 rounded teaspoon) of ricotta into the center of the batter in each well; reserve the remaining ricotta for serving. Cover the mold with its lid or aluminum foil and place it on the trivet.
5. Lock the lid into place. Select Pressure Cook and cook on high pressure for 7 minutes. When the cooking is complete, allow the pressure to release naturally for 7 minutes, then quick release any remaining pressure and remove the lid. Remove the egg mold.
6. In a small bowl, combine the lemon juice and maple syrup.
7. Serve 2 pancake bites with 1 tablespoon of maple-lemon syrup, 2 tablespoons of the reserved ricotta, and ½ cup of blueberries.

Nutrition Info:
- Per Serving: Calories: 193 ; Fat: 4 g ;Cholesterol: 51 mg ;Sodium: 194 mg

Apple Spiced Muffins

Servings: 8
Cooking Time: 15 Min
Ingredients:
- 1¾ cups whole-wheat flour
- ½ tsp baking powder
- 2 tbsp ground cinnamon
- 1½ tsp allspice
- 3 large free-range eggs
- ¾ cup fat free plain yogurt
- ¾ cup unsweetened applesauce
- 4 tbsp raisins
- 3 cups honey crisp apples, peeled, cored, and cut into bite-size pieces

Directions:
1. Heat the oven to 400°F gas mark 6. Line a muffin tin with paper liners.
2. In a medium sized mixing bowl, add the whole-wheat flour, baking powder, ground cinnamon, and allspice, mix until well blended.
3. In a large sized mixing bowl, add the large eggs, plain yogurt, unsweetened applesauce, and raisins.
4. Use a hand whisk, to fold half of the dry ingredients into the wet ingredients, then fold in the remaining flour mixture. Add the apple pieces and mix until fully incorporated.
5. Spoon the batter evenly into the prepared muffin tin. Bake for 15 minutes, or until a toothpick inserted comes out clean.
6. Serve warm or allow to cool completely before storing it in an airtight container.

Nutrition Info:
- Per Serving: Calories: 168 ; Fat: 3 g ;Cholesterol: 63 mg ;Sodium: 63 mg

Almond Rice Breakfast Pudding

Servings: 8
Cooking Time: 6 To 8 Hours
Ingredients:
- Nonstick cooking spray
- 6 cups low-fat or fat-free milk, or plant-based milk
- 2 cups long-grain brown rice
- 1 cup raisins
- 1 ripe banana, mashed
- 1 tablespoon honey, maple syrup, or sweetener of choice
- 2 teaspoons vanilla extract
- 1 teaspoon ground cinnamon
- ½ cup chopped almonds

Directions:
1. Spray the inside of a 6-quart slow cooker with the cooking spray. Combine the milk, rice, raisins, banana, honey, vanilla, and cinnamon. Cover and cook on low for 6 to 8 hours.
2. Serve hot. Top the rice with the chopped almonds and additional milk and sweetener, if desired.

Nutrition Info:
- Per Serving: Calories: 393 ; Fat: 8 g ;Cholesterol: 11 mg ;Sodium: 115 mg

Breakfast Burrito

Servings: 4
Cooking Time: 15 Minutes
Ingredients:
- 2 teaspoons olive oil
- ¼ teaspoon ground cumin
- ¼ teaspoon ground coriander
- ½ teaspoon garlic powder
- 4 ounces extra-firm tofu, diced
- ½ teaspoon low-sodium soy sauce
- 1½ cups water
- Nonstick cooking spray
- 3 medium eggs
- ¼ cup plus 2 tablespoons plain low-fat Greek yogurt
- 1 small red bell pepper, thinly sliced
- 1 small green bell pepper, thinly sliced
- 4 reduced-sodium flour tortillas
- 2 loose cups baby arugula

Directions:
1. Select Sauté and wait 30 seconds for the Instant Pot to warm. Pour in the oil and heat for 30 seconds, until it sizzles. Stir in the cumin, coriander, and garlic powder and cook for 30 seconds, until the aromas release. Add the tofu and cook for 1 minute. Transfer the tofu mixture to a bowl and stir in the soy sauce. Set aside.

2. Pour 1½ cups of water into the Instant Pot and set the trivet in the center. Coat a 6-inch round cake pan with nonstick spray.

3. In a medium bowl, whisk together the eggs, ¼ cup of yogurt, and the bell peppers. Pour the egg mixture into the prepared cake pan and cover with aluminum foil, then place the cake pan on the trivet.

4. Lock the lid into place. Select Pressure Cook and cook on high pressure for 15 minutes.

5. While the eggs are cooking, spread an even layer of the remaining 2 tablespoons yogurt onto each tortilla.

6. When the cooking is complete, allow the pressure to release naturally for 10 minutes, then quick release any remaining pressure and remove the lid.

7. Stir the egg mixture with a fork to give it a "scrambled egg" texture. Divide the egg mixture and tofu evenly over the tortillas, then top evenly with the arugula. Working with one at a time, fold in the sides of the tortillas and roll up to enclose the filling.

8. Divide the burritos among four plates and serve.

Nutrition Info:
- Per Serving: Calories: 252 ; Fat: 10 g ;Cholesterol: 125 mg ;Sodium: 285 mg

Raisin Cashew Oats

Servings: 4

Ingredients:
- 1 cup rolled oats
- 1 cup unsweetened cashew milk
- 2 tbsp flaxseeds
- 2 cups raisins
- ½ cup unsalted cashew nuts, chopped

Directions:

1. Divide the rolled oats, cashew milk, and flaxseeds into 4 small containers, mix well. Cover and place in the fridge overnight.

2. Once ready to serve, add ½ cup of raisins and 2 tbsp chopped cashew nuts per serving.

Nutrition Info:
- Per Serving: Calories:338 ; Fat: 16g ;Cholesterol: 0mg ;Sodium: 60mg

Spinach And Feta Frittata

Servings: 4

Cooking Time: 30 Min

Ingredients:
- 2 tablespoons extra-virgin olive oil
- ½ cup finely chopped onions
- 8 large eggs
- ¼ teaspoon black pepper
- 3 cups spinach, roughly chopped
- ½ cup roughly chopped Simple Roasted Peppers or jarred roasted red peppers
- ⅓ cup crumbled feta cheese

Directions:

1. Preheat the oven to 350°F.

2. Heat the oil in an 8- to 10-inch oven-safe skillet over medium-high heat. When hot, add the onion. Cook, stirring, until softened, about 5 minutes.

3. Meanwhile, in a large bowl, whisk together the eggs and pepper.

4. Add the spinach to the skillet, cover, and cook until slightly wilted, 1 to 2 minutes. Stir in the red peppers and cook for 1 to 2 minutes more. Lower the heat to medium, and add the eggs. Stir briefly to combine. Sprinkle the feta cheese on top.

5. Slide the skillet into the oven. Bake until the eggs are just set, about 15 minutes.

Nutrition Info:
- Per Serving: Calories: 254 ; Fat: 19 g ;Cholesterol: 383 mg ;Sodium: 418 mg

Potato, Pepper, And Egg Breakfast Casserole

Servings: 8
Cooking Time: 7 To 8 Hours

Ingredients:
- 12 large eggs
- 1 cup low-fat milk
- ¼ teaspoon dried mustard
- ½ teaspoon garlic powder
- ½ teaspoon salt
- ½ teaspoon freshly ground black pepper
- Nonstick cooking spray
- 1 (30-ounce) bag frozen hash browns, thawed in the refrigerator

- 1 (14-ounce) bag frozen peppers and onions, thawed in the refrigerator
- 6 ounces (1½ cups) 2% shredded Cheddar cheese

Directions:
1. In a large bowl, whisk together the eggs, milk, dried mustard, garlic powder, salt, and pepper.
2. Spray the bowl a 6-quart slow cooker with the cooking spray. Layer one-third of the hash browns in the slow cooker followed by one-third of the peppers and onions, then one-third of the cheese. Repeat the layers two more times.
3. Slowly pour the egg mixture over the top. Cover and cook on low for 7 to 8 hours.
4. Cut into 8 wedges and serve hot.

Nutrition Info:
- Per Serving: Calories: 340 ; Fat: 18 g ;Cholesterol: 296 mg ;Sodium: 421 mg

Soft-Boiled Egg Bites With Apricot Cheese Toasts

Servings: 4
Cooking Time: 3 Minutes
Ingredients:
- 4 slices whole-grain bread, toasted
- ½ cup low-fat ricotta
- ¼ cup plus 2 tablespoons water
- 7 or 8 medium apricots, pitted and sliced
- 1 tablespoon honey
- 1 cinnamon stick
- Nonstick cooking spray
- 4 medium eggs

Directions:
1. Divide the toast among four plates and spread 2 tablespoons of ricotta on each. Set aside.
2. Combine the water, apricots, honey, and cinnamon stick in the Instant Pot. Place an upside-down ramekin in the center and set the trivet on top, so that it's raised at least 1 inch above the fruit mixture.
3. Coat a 7-cup silicone egg mold with nonstick spray. Crack each egg into a well in the mold and carefully place the mold on the trivet.
4. Lock the lid into place. Select Pressure Cook and cook on high pressure for 3 minutes. When the cooking is complete, quick release the pressure. Remove the lid and lift out the egg mold, trivet, and ramekin. The egg yolks should be soft and sticky; nearly set, but not firm. Discard the cinnamon stick from the apricot mixture.
5. Use a spoon to transfer one egg bite to each ricotta-topped toast, then scoop ¼ cup of the apricot mixture over each piece of toast and serve.

Nutrition Info:
- Per Serving: Calories: 215 ; Fat: 8 g ;Cholesterol: 177 mg ;Sodium: 277 mg

Chapter 3 Poultry And Meat Mains Recipes

Southwest Steak Skillet

Servings: 4
Cooking Time: 25 Min
Ingredients:
- ⅔ cup uncooked quinoa
- 1 tablespoon canola or sunflower oil
- 12 ounces top sirloin beef, trimmed and thinly sliced
- ½ red onion, chopped
- 1 green bell pepper, seeded and chopped
- 1 cup no-salt-added black beans, rinsed and drained
- ⅔ cup reduced-sodium chicken broth
- 1 tablespoon Salt-Free Southwest Seasoning Mix or Mrs. Dash, plus more if needed
- 1 avocado, peeled, pitted, and diced
- ½ cup Fresh Tomato Salsa or lower-sodium store-bought salsa

Directions:
1. Cook the quinoa according to the package directions.
2. Meanwhile, heat the oil in a heavy skillet over medium-high heat. When it is hot, cook the steak slices until just cooked through, 3 to 4 minutes. Transfer to a plate.
3. Sauté the onion and pepper in the pan drippings until soft, 4 to 5 minutes. Turn the heat down to medium, if needed, to prevent them from burning. Add the black beans, broth, and Southwest seasoning. Turn the heat down to medium, cover, and cook, for 5 minutes.
4. Stir in the cooked quinoa when it is ready. Return the steak to the pan. Taste and add more Southwest Seasoning, if desired. Garnish with avocado and salsa.

Nutrition Info:
- Per Serving: Calories: 440; Fat: 22 g ;Cholesterol: 59 mg ;Sodium: 158 mg

Grilled Garlic-Lime Chicken

Servings: 4
Cooking Time: 30 Min
Ingredients:
- 1 pound boneless, skinless chicken breasts
- 2 tablespoons canola or sunflower oil, plus more for oiling the grill
- Zest and juice of 1 lime
- 2 garlic cloves, minced
- Freshly ground black pepper

Directions:
1. To cook on a grill
2. Preheat the grill to medium-high.
3. Arrange the chicken in a single layer in a shallow dish. Drizzle with the oil and lime juice. Sprinkle with the lime zest. Top with the garlic and pepper. Toss gently to mix the flavors and coat the chicken. Let the chicken marinate for at least 10 minutes.
4. Lightly coat the grill rack with oil. Transfer the chicken to the grill and cook until a meat thermometer reads 165°F, 4 to 5 minutes on each side. It should be opaque with mostly clear juices. Allow the chicken to rest for at least 5 minutes before cutting it.
5. To cook under the broiler
6. Set an oven rack 4 to 5 inches from the broiler, and preheat the broiler to high. Line a rimmed baking sheet with aluminum foil.
7. Cut each breast in half horizontally to make 2 thin cutlets. Press down to flatten. Arrange the chicken in a single layer in a shallow dish. Drizzle with the oil and lime juice. Sprinkle with the lime zest. Top with the garlic and pepper. Toss gently to mix the flavors and coat the chicken. Let the chicken marinate for at least 10 minutes.
8. Transfer the cutlets to the baking sheet. Broil, turning once, until the chicken is lightly browned on both sides and cooked to an internal temperature of 165°F, 4 to 5 minutes per side. It should be opaque with mostly clear juices. Allow the chicken to rest for at least 5 minutes before cutting it.

Nutrition Info:
- Per Serving: Calories: 202 ; Fat: 10 g ;Cholesterol: 83mg ;Sodium: 51 mg

Pineapple Chicken

Servings: 4
Cooking Time: 30 Min
Ingredients:
- Aluminum foil
- 1 lb. chicken breasts, boneless and skinless
- 2 tbsp olive oil, plus extra for frying
- 1 (20 oz) can crushed pineapple, drained
- 1 tbsp garlic, minced
- Ground black pepper

Directions:
1. Heat the broiler to high, and place the oven rack 4 to 5 inches from the broiler. Line a baking sheet with aluminum foil.
2. Slice each chicken breast in half horizontally, to make 2 thin cutlets. Place the cut chicken breasts in a large mixing bowl.
3. Add the olive oil, crushed pineapple, minced garlic and ground black pepper, and mix to combine. Allow the chicken to marinate for 10 minutes.
4. Transfer the chicken cutlets and the crushed pineapple to the baking sheet. Broil for 4 to 5 minutes per side, turning once, until the chicken is lightly browned on both sides, and fully cooked.
5. Allow the chicken to rest for 5 minutes before cutting and serving it.

Nutrition Info:
- Per Serving: Calories: 202 ; Fat: 10 g ;Cholesterol: 83 mg ;Sodium: 51 mg

Red Curry Beef Bowls

Servings: 4
Cooking Time: 5 Minutes
Ingredients:
- Nonstick cooking spray
- 6 ounces beef tenderloin or sirloin, cut into thin strips
- 1 medium yellow onion, diced
- 1 medium green bell pepper, diced
- 2 shishito peppers, seeded and finely sliced
- 1 cup shredded carrots
- ½ cup low-sodium marinara sauce
- 1½ tablespoons fish sauce
- 1 tablespoon crushed garlic
- 1 teaspoon grated fresh ginger
- 1 tablespoon ground cumin
- 1 tablespoon ground coriander
- ¾ cup uncooked brown rice
- 1½ cups water

Directions:
1. Select Sauté and wait 30 seconds for the Instant Pot to warm. Lightly coat the inner pot with nonstick spray and heat for 30 seconds. Insert the beef and onion and cook, stirring occasionally, for 3 minutes, until the beef is nearly browned. Add the bell and shishito peppers. Sauté for 2 to 3 minutes more.
2. Add the carrots, marinara, fish sauce, garlic, ginger, cumin, coriander, brown rice, and water (make sure the water covers the rice and add more if needed).
3. Lock the lid into place. Select Pressure Cook and cook on high pressure for 5 minutes. When the cooking is complete, allow the pressure to release naturally for 10 minutes, then quick release any remaining pressure and remove the lid.
4. Stir well and divide among four bowls.

Nutrition Info:
- Per Serving: Calories: 243 ; Fat: 5 g ;Cholesterol: 33 mg ;Sodium: 556 mg

Apple Pork Stir-Fry

Servings: 4
Cooking Time: 30 Min
Ingredients:
- 1 (1 lb.) boneless pork tenderloin
- ¼ tsp fine sea salt
- Ground black pepper
- 3 tbsp olive oil, divided
- 2 tsp ginger, grated
- 1 tbsp garlic, crushed
- 1 medium red bell pepper, seeded and chopped
- 1 medium green bell pepper, seeded and chopped
- 2 medium granny smith apples, cored and cut into chunks
- 2 tbsp apple cider vinegar
- 1½ tbsp reduced-sodium tamari

- 1 cup sweet peas

Directions:
1. Cut the pork tenderloin in half, lengthwise, and thinly slice each half. Season with fine sea salt and ground black pepper.
2. Heat 1 tbsp olive oil in a large, heavy bottom pan over high heat. Once hot, add the pork slices. Fry on both sides for 3 to 5 minutes, until lightly browned.
3. Add the grated ginger and crushed garlic, and cook for 1 minute, until soft. Transfer to a plate. Add the chopped red bell pepper, chopped green bell pepper, and apple chunks to the pan, and cook for 3 to 4 minutes, until softened.
4. In a small mixing bowl, combine the apple cider vinegar, tamari, and the remaining 2 tbsp olive oil, and whisk until mixed.
5. Add the vinegar mixture to the apple mixture. Cook for about 2 minutes, until fully incorporated. Add the sweet peas and pork slices, and cook until warmed through. Serve warm.

Nutrition Info:
- Per Serving: Calories: 306 ; Fat: 14 g ;Cholesterol:74 mg ;Sodium: 451 mg

Rosemary Lemon Chicken With Vegetables

Servings: 6
Cooking Time: 7 To 8 Hours
Ingredients:
- 1 pound baby potatoes, halved
- 6 medium carrots, peeled and sliced
- 2 medium onions, sliced
- Freshly ground black pepper
- 3 teaspoons dried rosemary, divided
- 2 pounds boneless, skinless chicken breasts
- Juice of 2 lemons (about ½ cup)
- 1 cup Chicken Stock (here) or low-sodium chicken broth
- 4 fresh rosemary sprigs
- 4 garlic cloves, minced

Directions:
1. Place the potatoes, carrots, and onions in the bottom of the slow cooker. Sprinkle them with black pepper and 1½ teaspoons of dried rosemary. Place the chicken on top of the vegetables.
2. Pour the lemon juice and stock over the chicken and vegetables. Place the fresh rosemary and garlic on top of the chicken. Cover and cook on low for 7 to 8 hours, until the chicken is cooked through and vegetables are tender.
3. Remove and discard the rosemary sprigs. Serve hot.

Nutrition Info:
- Per Serving: Calories: 288; Fat: 5 g ;Cholesterol: 87 mg ;Sodium: 108 mg

Blueberry, Pistachio, And Parsley Chicken

Servings: 2
Cooking Time: 25 Minutes
Ingredients:
- ½ cup blueberries
- 2 tablespoons shelled unsalted raw pistachios
- ¼ cup chopped fresh parsley
- 2 tablespoons balsamic vinegar
- ¼ teaspoon freshly ground black pepper
- 2 (4-ounce) pieces of chicken

Directions:
1. Preheat the oven to 375°F. Line a baking dish with parchment paper.
2. In a medium mixing bowl, mix the blueberries, pistachios, parsley, vinegar, and pepper until well combined.
3. Put the chicken in the baking dish and pour the blueberry mixture on top. Bake for 20 to 25 minutes, depending on the thickness of the chicken (20 minutes for 1-inch-thick chicken, 25 minutes for 2-inch-thick chicken), until the juices are caramelized and the inside of the chicken has cooked through. Serve on a plate with a side dish of your choice. Store in the refrigerator in an airtight container for up to 3 days.

Nutrition Info:
- Per Serving: Calories: 212 ; Fat: 7 g ;Cholesterol: 80 mg ;Sodium: 58 mg

Ras El Hanout Lamb Stew

Servings: 4
Cooking Time: 50 Minutes
Ingredients:
- 2 tablespoons extra-virgin olive oil
- 1 pound boneless lamb shoulder (stew meat), diced
- 1 large onion, chopped
- 2 carrots, chopped
- 1 (15-ounce) can chickpeas, drained and rinsed
- 2 teaspoons ras el hanout
- 4 cups water
- ½ teaspoon salt
- ¼ teaspoon freshly ground black pepper

Directions:
1. In a large pot, heat the oil over medium-high heat.
2. Add the lamb, and brown on all sides for 3 to 5 minutes per side. Leaving the juices in the pot, transfer the lamb to a plate.
3. Add the onion and carrots to the pot. Cook for 3 to 5 minutes, or until softened and browned.
4. Add the chickpeas and ras el hanout. Mix well.
5. Add the lamb back to the pot, along with any juices that have collected on the plate. Add the water, and bring to a boil.
6. Reduce the heat to low. Cover the pot, and simmer for 30 to 40 minutes, or until the lamb is tender. Remove from the heat. Season with the salt and pepper.

Nutrition Info:
- Per Serving: Calories:399 ; Fat: 25 g ;Cholesterol: 0mg ;Sodium: 501 mg

No-Fuss Turkey Breast

Servings: 8
Cooking Time: 7 To 8 Hours
Ingredients:
- 1 (4- to 5-pound) bone-in turkey breast, skin removed, thawed (if frozen)
- 1 tablespoon extra-virgin olive oil
- 2 teaspoons dried thyme
- 1 teaspoon paprika
- 1 teaspoon dried garlic
- Freshly ground black pepper
- Nonstick cooking spray
- 2 cups Brussels sprouts, halved
- 2 onions, cut into large chunks, divided
- 4 celery ribs, cut into 3-inch lengths
- 12 baby carrots
- 1 cup Turkey Stock (here) or low-sodium turkey broth
- 4 or 5 fresh thyme sprigs (optional)

Directions:
1. Brush the turkey with the olive oil.
2. In a small bowl, mix together the dried thyme, paprika, garlic, and black pepper. Rub the mixture all over the turkey.
3. Spray a 6-quart slow cooker with the cooking spray. Add the Brussels sprouts, chunks of 1 onion, celery, and carrots, to the slow cooker. Pour the broth over the vegetables. Place the turkey breast on top of the vegetables, making sure it does not touch the bottom of the slow cooker. Cover the turkey with the chunks of the second onion and the fresh thyme (if using).
4. Cover and cook on low for 7 to 8 hours, or until the turkey's internal temperature reaches 165 °F.
5. Let the turkey rest for 10 minutes before carving. Serve hot, with fresh Cranberry Sauce (here) and your favorite fixings.

Nutrition Info:
- Per Serving: Calories: 367 ; Fat: 10 g ;Cholesterol: 147 mg ;Sodium: 380 mg

Balsamic Berry Chicken

Servings: 2
Cooking Time: 30 Min
Ingredients:
- Aluminum foil
- ½ cup blueberries
- 2 tbsp pine nuts
- ¼ cup basil, finely chopped
- 2 tbsp balsamic vinegar
- ¼ tsp ground black pepper
- 2 (4 oz) chicken breasts, butterflied

Directions:
1. Heat the oven to 375°F, gas mark 5. Line a medium-sized baking dish with aluminum foil.

2. In a medium-sized mixing bowl, add together the blueberries, pine nuts, chopped basil, balsamic vinegar, and ground black pepper. Mix until well combined.
3. Place the chicken pieces in the baking dish, and pour the blueberry mixture on top.
4. Bake for 20 to 30 minutes, or until the juices are caramelized, and the inside of the chicken is fully cooked.
5. Serve warm, with a side dish of your choice.

Nutrition Info:
- Per Serving: Calories: 212 ; Fat: 7 g ;Cholesterol: 80 mg ;Sodium: 58 mg

Tuscan Turkey, White Beans, And Asparagus

Servings: 8
Cooking Time: 7 To 8 Hours
Ingredients:
- Nonstick cooking spray
- 1 pound dried cannellini beans, soaked overnight and drained
- 3 cups Turkey Stock (here) or low-sodium turkey stock
- 3 tablespoons extra-virgin olive oil
- 6 garlic cloves, minced
- 1 teaspoon dried sage
- 1 teaspoon dried rosemary
- Freshly ground black pepper
- 2 pounds turkey thighs, skin removed
- 3 cups chopped asparagus

Directions:
1. Spray a 6-quart slow cooker with the cooking spray. Put the beans in the slow cooker and add the broth.
2. In a small bowl, stir together the olive oil, garlic, sage, rosemary, and black pepper. Press this mixture firmly into the turkey thighs. Place the turkey on top of the beans in the slow cooker. Cover and cook on low for 7 to 8 hours, until the beans are tender and the turkey reaches an internal temperature of 165°F.
3. Remove the turkey from the slow cooker and increase the heat to high. Add the asparagus and cook for 15 to 20 minutes, or until the asparagus is bright green and crisp tender.
4. While the asparagus is cooking, remove the turkey meat from the bones. To serve, ladle the bean and asparagus mixture into bowls and top with the turkey meat.

Nutrition Info:
- Per Serving: Calories: 326 ; Fat: 12 g ;Cholesterol: 70 mg ;Sodium: 72 mg

Buffalo-Seasoned Chicken Wrap

Servings: 6
Cooking Time: 7 To 8 Hours
Ingredients:
- For the chicken
- Nonstick cooking spray
- 2 pounds boneless, skinless chicken breasts
- 2 medium celery stalks, chopped
- 1 medium onion, chopped
- 2 garlic cloves, minced
- 2 cups Chicken Stock (here) low-sodium chicken broth
- ½ cup cayenne hot sauce
- 2 tablespoons honey
- For the blue-cheese sauce
- ¼ cup plain nonfat Greek yogurt
- ¼ cup blue cheese crumbles
- ¼ cup low-fat or fat-free milk, or plant-based milk (or more as needed)
- 1 tablespoon freshly squeezed lemon juice
- Cayenne hot sauce to taste
- To serve
- 8 to 16 large lettuce leaves, such as Bibb or romaine
- 2 cups shredded carrots

Directions:
1. To make the chicken
2. Spray the inside of a 6-quart slow cooker with cooking spray. Place the chicken in the slow cooker and top it with the celery, onion, and garlic.
3. In a medium bowl, whisk together the stock, hot sauce, and honey. Pour this over the chicken. Cover and cook on low for 6 to 8 hours.
4. Remove the chicken and shred it using two forks. Stir the shredded chicken back into the Buffalo sauce and let it soak up the flavors for 5 to 10 minutes.
5. To make the blue-cheese sauce

6. Whisk together the yogurt, blue cheese, milk, lemon juice, and hot sauce.
7. To serve
8. To serve, wrap the chicken, shredded carrots, and blue-cheese sauce in 8 large (or 16 small) lettuce leaves. Add additional hot sauce, if desired.

Nutrition Info:
- Per Serving: Calories: 273 ; Fat: 7 g ;Cholesterol: 92 mg ;Sodium: 211 mg

Tahini And Turmeric Chicken Salad

Servings: 2
Cooking Time: 10 Minutes
Ingredients:
- 2 teaspoons avocado oil
- 2 large garlic cloves, minced
- 1 (8-ounce) chicken breast, cubed
- 3 tablespoons unsalted tahini
- ½ teaspoon ground turmeric
- ¼ teaspoon freshly ground black pepper
- 1 tablespoon lemon juice
- 2 tablespoons water
- 2 celery stalks, diced
- 1 Honeycrisp apple, cut into ½-inch pieces

Directions:
1. In a medium skillet, heat the oil and garlic over medium heat for 2 minutes, until the garlic is sizzling and translucent.
2. Add the chicken breast and cook for 4 minutes on one side, until the chicken is ⅔ white around the bottom. Flip and cook for another 2 minutes, until the browned chicken is lightly golden and cooked through.
3. In a large mixing bowl, add the tahini, turmeric, pepper, lemon juice, and water and combine thoroughly. Add in the browned chicken breast, celery, and apples and mix well.
4. Enjoy over a lettuce wrap, salad, or on one or two slices of whole wheat bread. Store in an airtight container in the refrigerator for up to 3 days.

Nutrition Info:
- Per Serving: Calories: 366 ; Fat: 20 g ;Cholesterol: 80 mg ;Sodium: 112 mg

Hawaiian Barbeque Chicken

Servings: 2
Cooking Time: 20 Minutes
Ingredients:
- 2 (4-ounce) chicken breasts, flattened 1-inch thick
- 2 teaspoons sesame seeds
- 1 cup diced pineapple
- 1 cup diced green bell peppers
- 1 cup Barbeque Sauce

Directions:
1. Preheat the oven to 400°F. Line a baking sheet with parchment paper.
2. Place the chicken on the prepared baking sheet and top with sesame seeds. Surround the chicken with the pineapple and green peppers. Coat the chicken with barbeque sauce and cook for 10 to 15 minutes, until the pineapple is caramelized and the chicken is cooked through. Serve with a side of your choice, or store in an airtight container in the refrigerator for up to 3 days.

Nutrition Info:
- Per Serving: Calories: 327 ; Fat: 6 g ;Cholesterol: 80 mg ;Sodium: 206 mg

Turkey Burgers

Servings: 4
Cooking Time: 10 Minutes
Ingredients:
- 1 pound ground turkey
- ¼ cup crumbled feta cheese
- 2 tablespoons chopped fresh basil leaves
- 1 large egg
- 1 teaspoon Worcestershire sauce
- ¼ teaspoon freshly ground black pepper

Directions:
1. In a large bowl, combine the turkey, cheese, basil, egg, Worcestershire sauce, and pepper. Mix well, and form into 4 patties. Transfer to a plate.
2. Heat a large nonstick skillet over medium-high heat.

3. Add the patties, and cook for 3 to 4 minutes per side, or until browned and cooked through. Remove from the heat. Serve with your favorite burger toppings.

Nutrition Info:
- Per Serving: Calories: 214 ; Fat: 13 g ;Cholesterol: 0mg ;Sodium: 196 mg

Turkey Cauliflower Burgers

Servings: 4
Cooking Time: 15 Minutes
Ingredients:
- 2 cups cauliflower florets (about ½ medium cauliflower head)
- 1 small yellow onion, quartered
- 8 ounces frozen spinach, thawed
- 1 pound lean ground turkey
- 1½ teaspoons Mediterranean Seasoning Rub Blend

Directions:
1. Set an oven rack 6 inches from the broiler and preheat the oven to broil. Line a baking sheet with parchment paper.
2. In a blender, pulse the cauliflower and onion for 1 to 2 minutes, until they are minced.
3. In a large mixing bowl, combine the spinach, cauliflower and onion mixture, turkey, and the spice blend. Mix well and form into 8 medium patties and place them on the baking sheet.
4. Broil for 10 minutes on one side, flip when lightly golden and juicy, and then broil for 3 minutes on the other side until golden brown. Serve on a whole wheat bun with lettuce and tomato, on top of a salad, or in a collard green wrap. The burgers can be stored in the refrigerator in an airtight container for up to 3 days or frozen for up to 3 months.

Nutrition Info:
- Per Serving: Calories: 206 ; Fat: 10 g ;Cholesterol: 84 mg ;Sodium: 134 mg

Spicy Beef Roast

Servings: 6
Cooking Time: 30 Min
Ingredients:
- 1 tsp dried rosemary
- ½ tsp paprika
- ½ tsp red chili flakes
- ½ tsp cayenne pepper
- ½ tsp ground coriander
- ½ tsp onion powder
- ½ tsp garlic powder
- ¼ tsp fine sea salt
- ¼ tsp ground black pepper
- 1½ lb. beef tenderloin
- 1 tbsp avocado oil
- 3 bay leaves
- 3 thyme sprigs

Directions:
1. Heat the oven to 400ºF, gas mark 6.
2. In a small mixing bowl, add together the dried rosemary, paprika, red chili flakes, cayenne pepper, ground coriander, onion powder, garlic powder, fine sea salt, and ground black pepper. Mix to combine.
3. Rub the spice mixture all over the beef tenderloin.
4. In a large, oven-safe frying pan, heat the avocado oil over high heat. Add the bay leaves and thyme sprigs, and cook for 30 seconds, or until fragrant.
5. Add the tenderloin, and fry for 2 to 3 minutes on all sides until browned. Turn off the heat.
6. Place the oven safe frying pan in the oven, and cook for 15 to 20 minutes, or until the tenderloin is fully cooked. Remove from the oven, discard the bay leaves and thyme sprigs. Serve immediately.

Nutrition Info:
- Per Serving: Calories: 160 ; Fat: 6 g ;Cholesterol:0 mg ;Sodium: 157 mg

Asian Turkey Lettuce Wraps

Servings: 8
Cooking Time: 6 To 7 Hours
Ingredients:
- 2 pounds 93% lean ground turkey breast meat
- 1 (8-ounce) can water chestnuts, drained and sliced
- 2 red bell peppers, chopped
- 1 onion, finely chopped
- 1 cup frozen, shelled edamame
- 4 garlic cloves, minced
- 2 tablespoons low-sodium tamari
- 2 tablespoons rice wine vinegar
- 1 tablespoon grated fresh ginger
- 2 teaspoons sesame oil
- 1 teaspoon ground coriander
- 1 head romaine lettuce leaves
- 1 cup finely shredded carrot
- 1 cup finely shredded cabbage
- 4 tablespoons sesame seeds

Directions:
1. Crumble the ground turkey into a 6-quart slow cooker. Add the water chestnuts, bell peppers, onion, edamame, garlic, tamari, vinegar, ginger, sesame oil, and coriander and stir to combine. Cover and cook on low for 6 to 7 hours.
2. Wrap the meat mixture evenly in the lettuce leaves and top with the carrots, cabbage, and sesame seeds.

Nutrition Info:
- Per Serving: Calories: 249 ; Fat: 12 g ;Cholesterol: 80 mg ;Sodium: 240 mg

Red Beans, Sausage, And Rice

Servings: 4
Cooking Time: 30 Min
Ingredients:
- ¾ cup uncooked parboiled brown rice or 2 cups cooked brown rice
- 1 tablespoon canola or sunflower oil
- 6 ounces smoked andouille sausage, cut into bite-size pieces
- 1 onion, chopped
- 1 green bell pepper, seeded and chopped
- 1 red bell pepper, seeded and chopped
- 4 garlic cloves, minced
- 1 (28-ounce) can no-salt-added whole tomatoes
- 1 (15-ounce) can no-salt-added kidney beans, rinsed and drained
- 1 teaspoon ground cumin
- 1 teaspoon dried thyme
- ½ teaspoon red pepper flakes
- ¼ teaspoon freshly ground black pepper

Directions:
1. Start the rice cooking according to the package directions.
2. Meanwhile, heat the oil in a large, heavy skillet over medium-high heat. Add the sausage and cook until lightly browned, 3 to 4 minutes. Add the onion, bell peppers, and garlic, and cook until softened, 5 to 6 minutes.
3. Stir in the tomatoes with their juice, beans, cumin, thyme, red pepper flakes, and black pepper. Bring to a boil. Add the rice whether it's ready or not (including any water yet to be absorbed). Turn the heat down to medium-low, and cover. Simmer until the rice is fully cooked, 5 to 10 minutes.
4. Taste, and adjust the seasonings.

Nutrition Info:
- Per Serving: Calories: 395 ; Fat: 11 g ;Cholesterol: 26 mg ;Sodium: 337 mg

Indian Butter Chicken

Servings: 6
Cooking Time: 6 To 8 Hours
Ingredients:
- 2 pounds boneless, skinless chicken breasts, cut into 2-inch pieces
- 1 (14.5-ounce) can light coconut milk
- 1 (6-ounce) can tomato paste
- 1 onion, diced
- 1 red bell pepper, diced
- 4 garlic cloves, minced
- 2 tablespoons freshly squeezed lemon juice
- 1 tablespoon grated fresh ginger
- 2 teaspoons curry powder
- 2 teaspoons garam masala
- 1 cup nonfat plain yogurt, divided

Directions:
1. Combine the chicken, coconut milk, tomato paste, onion, bell pepper, garlic, lemon juice, ginger, curry powder, and garam masala juice in a 6-quart slow cooker. Cover and cook on low for 6 to 8 hours, until the chicken is cooked through and the vegetables are tender.
2. Fifteen minutes before serving, stir in ½ cup of yogurt.
3. Serve hot with a dollop of the remaining ½ cup of yogurt on each serving. If desired, serve over basmati or jasmine rice with a garnish of fresh cilantro.

Nutrition Info:
- Per Serving: Calories: 288 ; Fat: 9 g ;Cholesterol: 88 mg ;Sodium: 359 mg

Braised Beef

Servings: 6
Cooking Time: 1 Hour 15 Minutes
Ingredients:
- 1 tablespoon extra-virgin olive oil
- 1 onion, sliced
- 3 garlic cloves, minced
- 1½ pounds beef chuck roast, cut into 1-inch pieces
- 1 (28-ounce) can whole tomatoes
- ½ teaspoon freshly ground black pepper
- ¼ cup chopped fresh parsley

Directions:
1. Preheat the oven to 350°F.
2. In a large oven-safe pot, heat the oil over medium-high heat.
3. Add the onion, and cook for 3 to 5 minutes, or until slightly softened.
4. Add the garlic, and cook for 30 seconds, or until fragrant.
5. Add the roast, and cook for 5 to 6 minutes, browning it on all sides.
6. Add the tomatoes with their juices, salt, and pepper. Bring to a boil. Turn off the heat.
7. Cover the pot with a lid, and transfer to the oven. Cook, stirring occasionally and scraping up the browned bits off the bottom of the pot, for 1 hour, or until the meat is tender. Remove from the oven. Let rest for 10 minutes.
8. Using a large spoon, skim any fat from the top of the mixture.
9. Serve the roast topped with the parsley.

Nutrition Info:
- Per Serving: Calories: 202 ; Fat: 9 g ;Cholesterol: 0mg ;Sodium: 460 mg

Mushroom Bolognese

Servings: 6
Cooking Time: 30 Min
Ingredients:
- 1 pound extra-lean (7% fat) ground beef
- ½ teaspoon salt, divided (optional)
- Freshly ground black pepper
- 1 onion, chopped
- 3 garlic cloves, minced
- ½ cup uncooked split red lentils, rinsed
- 1 (28-ounce) can whole, no-salt-added tomatoes
- 1 pound sliced mushrooms
- ⅔ cup water
- 2 tablespoons tomato paste
- 1 tablespoon dried oregano

Directions:
1. Heat a large sauté pan over medium heat. When the pan is hot, add the beef and sprinkle with ¼ teaspoon salt (if using) and the pepper. Do not stir the meat until it is browned on the bottom, 2 to 3 minutes. Add the onion and garlic, and stir periodically until the beef is no longer pink, 5 to 7 minutes.
2. Turn up the heat and add the lentils, tomatoes with their juice, mushrooms, water, tomato paste, and oregano. When it boils, reduce the heat to medium and simmer, stirring occasionally, until the lentils are soft, about 15 minutes.
3. Taste, and add an extra ¼ teaspoon of salt and pepper, if desired.

Nutrition Info:
- Per Serving: Calories: 225 ; Fat: 6 g ;Cholesterol: 48 mg ;Sodium: 266 mg

Chicken Lettuce Wrap With Peanut Dressing

Servings: 2
Cooking Time: 5 Minutes
Ingredients:
- 2 teaspoons avocado oil
- 2 garlic cloves, minced, divided
- ½ cup diced shallots
- 8 ounces lean ground chicken or turkey breast
- 1 teaspoon grated ginger
- 3 tablespoons unsalted peanut butter
- 4 tablespoons water
- 6 large butter lettuce leaves

Directions:
1. In a medium skillet, heat the oil over medium heat. Add 1 minced garlic clove and the shallots and cook for 1 to 2 minutes, until sizzling and translucent.
2. Add the ground chicken and break into pieces. Stir the ground meat until lightly golden and cooked through, about 5 minutes.
3. In a small mixing bowl, combine the ginger, remaining garlic clove, peanut butter, and water. Add to the chicken mixture on the stovetop. Cook for about 1 minute until all flavors have combined.
4. Divide the chicken mixture into the lettuce cups and serve. Alternatively, this dish can be stored in an airtight container in the refrigerator for up to 3 days.

Nutrition Info:
- Per Serving: Calories: 414 ; Fat: 21 g ;Cholesterol: 90 mg ;Sodium: 211 mg

Chicken Cacciatore

Servings: 4
Cooking Time: 35 Minutes
Ingredients:
- 2 tablespoons extra-virgin olive oil
- 4 bone-in chicken thighs, skin removed
- ¼ teaspoon salt
- ¼ teaspoon freshly ground black pepper
- 1 large onion, sliced
- 1 red bell pepper, cored and sliced
- 1 recipe Marinara Sauce

Directions:
1. In a large skillet, heat the oil over medium-high heat.
2. Season the chicken with the salt and pepper. Add the chicken to the skillet, and brown for 2 to 3 minutes per side. Transfer the chicken to a plate.
3. Add the onion and bell pepper to the skillet. Cook for 3 to 5 minutes, or until softened.
4. Add the marinara sauce, and mix well. Bring to a simmer.
5. Return the chicken to the skillet, and simmer for 20 minutes, or until cooked through. Remove from the heat.

Nutrition Info:
- Per Serving: Calories: 325 ; Fat: 20 g ;Cholesterol: 0mg ;Sodium: 482 mg

Salsa Verde Chicken

Servings: 6
Cooking Time: 5 To 6 Hours
Ingredients:
- Nonstick cooking spray
- 2 pounds boneless, skinless chicken breasts
- 2 cups salsa verde
- 1 (14.5-ounce) can no-salt-added fire-roasted tomatoes
- 1 (4-ounce) can green chiles
- 1 bell pepper (any color), chopped
- 2 teaspoons ground cumin
- 1 teaspoon dried oregano
- Freshly ground black pepper
- Optional toppings: chopped fresh cilantro, avocado slices, lime wedges, lettuce leaves

Directions:
1. Spray the inside of a 6-quart slow cooker with the cooking spray. Place the chicken in the bottom of the slow cooker. Add the salsa verde, tomatoes, chiles, bell pepper, cumin, oregano, and black pepper, and stir to combine. Cover and cook on low for 5 to 6 hours.
2. Remove the chicken and shred it using two forks. Stir the shredded chicken back into the slow cooker and taste to adjust seasonings.

3. Serve hot, with toppings such as chopped fresh cilantro, avocado slices, or lime wedges, if desired.

Nutrition Info:
- Per Serving: Calories: 257 ; Fat: 5 g ;Cholesterol: 87 mg ;Sodium: 646 mg

Beef And Vegetable Stew

Servings: 6
Cooking Time: 6 To 8 Hours
Ingredients:
- 1 tablespoon extra-virgin olive oil (optional)
- 2 pounds beef stew meat, cubed
- 4 cups Beef Stock (here) or low-sodium beef broth
- 1 (14-ounce) can no-salt-added diced tomatoes
- ½ pound baby potatoes, quartered
- ½ pound parsnips, peeled and cubed
- 4 medium carrots, chopped
- 2 cups green beans, fresh or frozen
- 1 medium onion, diced
- 2 celery stalks, diced
- 2 garlic cloves, minced
- 2 teaspoons dried thyme
- 3 tablespoons cold water
- 2 tablespoons cornstarch

Directions:
1. Optional step: Heat the oil in a large nonstick skillet over medium-high heat. Add the beef and cook until browned on all sides, 2 to 3 minutes. (If you choose not to brown the meat first, the olive oil does not need to be added to the slow cooker.)
2. Add the beef, stock, tomatoes, potatoes, parsnips, carrots, green beans, onion, celery, garlic, and thyme to a 6-quart slow cooker. Cover and cook on low for 6 to 8 hours.
3. With 30 minutes left to cook, combine the cold water and cornstarch, stirring until the cornstarch is dissolved. Stir this into the stew. Turn the slow cooker to the high setting and continue cooking until the stew is thickened.
4. Serve hot.

Nutrition Info:
- Per Serving: Calories: 354 ; Fat: 9 g;Cholesterol: 100 mg ;Sodium: 445 mg

Basil Pesto Chicken

Servings: 4
Cooking Time: 15 Min
Ingredients:
- 8 oz uncooked rotini pasta
- 1 lb. asparagus, woody ends removed, cut into bite-size pieces
- 1 tbsp coconut oil
- 12 oz boneless, skinless chicken breasts, cut into bite-size cubes
- 2 medium Roma tomatoes, chopped
- ½ cup basil pesto
- ¼ cup Parmesan cheese, grated

Directions:
1. Cook the rotini pasta according to the package instructions, or until al dente. Scoop out ½ cup of the cooking water, and keep to one side. Add the asparagus pieces to the pasta when it reaches the 4 minutes left mark. Allow to boil.
2. In a large, heavy bottom pan, heat the coconut oil over medium-high heat. Fry the cubed chicken breasts for 5 to 10 minutes, or until cooked through. Stir in the chopped tomatoes, and remove the pan from the heat.
3. Drain the pasta and asparagus in a colander, and return them to the stockpot.
4. Toss the pasta and asparagus with the basil pesto, and ¼ cup of the reserved cooking water. Add the cooked chicken mixture, and more cooking water if needed.
5. Top with the grated Parmesan cheese, and serve hot.

Nutrition Info:
- Per Serving: Calories: 485 ; Fat: 17 g ;Cholesterol: 68mg ;Sodium: 201mg

Turkey And Mushroom Wild Rice Casserole

Servings: 8
Cooking Time: 7 To 8 Hours
Ingredients:
- Nonstick cooking spray
- 1 cup cold low-fat or fat-free milk, or plant-based milk
- 3 tablespoons extra-virgin olive oil
- 3 tablespoons cornstarch

- 6 cups Turkey Stock (here) or low-sodium turkey broth, divided
- 2 pounds turkey breast tenderloin, cut into ¾-inch pieces
- 2 cups wild rice, rinsed and drained
- 1 onion, chopped
- 1 cup sliced carrot
- 1 cup sliced celery
- 1 cup sliced button mushrooms
- 1 teaspoon dried tarragon
- ¼ teaspoon freshly ground black pepper
- ½ cup sliced almonds
- ½ cup chopped scallions, for garnish (optional)

Directions:
1. Spray the inside of a 6-quart slow cooker with the cooking spray.
2. In a small bowl, whisk together the cold milk, olive oil, and cornstarch. Add 1 cup of broth and whisk to combine. Pour this mixture into the slow cooker.
3. Add the turkey, rice, onion, carrot, celery, mushrooms, tarragon, and black pepper to the slow cooker. Pour in the remaining 5 cups of broth and stir to combine. Cover and cook on low for 7 to 8 hours, until vegetables are tender, the rice has absorbed the liquid, and the turkey is cooked through.
4. Serve hot, garnished with the sliced almonds and scallions, if using.

Nutrition Info:
- Per Serving: Calories: 420 ; Fat: 9 g ;Cholesterol: 70 mg ;Sodium: 158 mg

Parmesan Pork Chops

Servings: 4
Cooking Time: 25 Min
Ingredients:
- 2 tbsp avocado oil
- 4 thick pork chops, fat trimmed
- ½ red onion, chopped
- 1½ cups couscous
- 2½ cups water
- ½ cup sun-dried tomatoes, chopped
- 3 cups kale, finely chopped
- ¼ cup parmesan cheese, grated

Directions:
1. Heat the avocado oil in a large, heavy bottom pan, over high heat.
2. Add the pork chops, and fry for 1½ minutes on each side, until browned. Transfer to a plate.
3. Reduce the heat to medium. Add the chopped onion, and cook for 3 to 5 minutes, until softened.
4. Add the couscous, and cook for 1 to 2 minutes, until browned.
5. Pour in the water, and deglaze the pan by scraping the bottom.
6. Add the chopped sun-dried tomatoes, and allow to simmer for 5 minutes.
7. Return the pork chops to the pan, cover, and reduce the heat to low. Cook for 6 to 8 minutes, or until the chops are fully cooked, and the couscous is tender.
8. Remove from the heat, and mix in the grated parmesan cheese and chopped kale, stirring until the kale is wilted. Serve warm.

Nutrition Info:
- Per Serving: Calories: 484; Fat: 18 g ;Cholesterol:0mg ;Sodium: 103 mg

Spicy Turkey Wraps

Servings: 4
Cooking Time: 20 Min
Ingredients:
- For the sauce:
- 1 small jalapeno, halved, seeds removed, minced
- 1 tbsp garlic, crushed
- 3 tbsp organic honey
- ½ cup water
- ½ tbsp low-sodium soy sauce
- 2 tbsp lemon juice
- For the turkey:
- 1 tbsp sesame oil
- 1 tbsp ginger, grated
- 1 tbsp garlic, crushed
- 12 oz boneless, skinless turkey breasts, cut into strips
- 1 tbsp low-sodium soy sauce
- 1 tbsp sesame seeds

- For the wrap:
- 4 large lettuce leaves
- 8 basil leaves, roughly chopped
- 2 cups napa cabbage, julienned

Directions:
1. For the sauce:
2. In a medium-sized stockpot, combine the minced jalapeno, crushed garlic, organic honey, water, soy sauce, and lemon juice. Mix, and bring to a boil over high heat. Remove from the heat, and allow to sit for 3 to 5 minutes. Chill the sauce in the fridge for 15 minutes, or until cold.
3. For the turkey:
4. Heat the sesame oil in a large, heavy bottom pan, over medium heat. Add the grated ginger and crushed garlic, and fry for 30 seconds, until lightly cooked.
5. Add the turkey strips, and fry for 5 to 8 minutes, or until fully cooked. Add the soy sauce and sesame seeds. Allow to simmer. Remove from the heat, and cover with a lid.
6. For the wrap:
7. Place a large lettuce leaf on a plate, and add ½ cup of the turkey mixture, 1 tsp chopped basil, and ½ cup julienned napa cabbage. Fold the lettuce wrap together. Divide the sauce between the wraps.

Nutrition Info:
- Per Serving: Calories: 242 ; Fat: 10 g ;Cholesterol: 47 mg ;Sodium: 393 mg

Pan-Seared Pork Medallions With Pears

Servings: 4
Cooking Time: 30 Min
Ingredients:
- 2 cups water
- 1 cup uncooked pearl barley
- 1 (1-pound) boneless pork tenderloin roast
- ½ teaspoon kosher salt
- Freshly ground black pepper
- 1 tablespoon canola or sunflower oil
- 3 celery stalks, chopped
- 2 shallots, chopped
- 1 garlic clove, minced
- 1 tablespoon unsalted butter
- ½ teaspoon dried rosemary
- ¼ teaspoon ground ginger
- 1 tablespoon all-purpose flour
- 1 cup reduced-sodium chicken broth
- 1 (15-ounce) can sliced pears, drained

Directions:
1. Bring the water to a boil in a large pot over high heat. Add the barley. Cover the pot, reduce the heat, and simmer for 25 minutes or until tender.
2. Meanwhile, trim the tenderloin of any silverskin, and pat it dry. Slice the tenderloin into ½-inch-thick medallions. Sprinkle with salt and pepper.
3. Heat the oil in a large skillet over medium-high heat. When it is hot, cook the pork until it is browned on both sides, about 3 minutes per side. Transfer to a plate, and tent with aluminum foil.
4. Add the celery, shallots, garlic, butter, rosemary, and ginger to the skillet, and sauté for 2 to 3 minutes. Stir in the flour until blended. Then gradually add the broth, stirring constantly, until the mixture comes to a boil. Cook and stir for 1 minute, until thickened.
5. Add the pears, and return the pork to the skillet. Taste and adjust the seasoning, if needed. Serve the pork, pears, and sauce over the barley.

Nutrition Info:
- Per Serving: Calories: 438 ; Fat: 10 g ;Cholesterol: 82 mg ;Sodium: 362mg

Lemon-Basil Chicken With Baby Bell Peppers

Servings: 2
Cooking Time: 20 Minutes
Ingredients:
- 8 ounces chicken breast, cubed
- 4 cups baby bell peppers
- ¾ teaspoon Mediterranean Seasoning Rub Blend
- 2 heaping tablespoons chopped fresh basil
- 2 tablespoons lemon juice
- 1 teaspoon avocado oil

Directions:

1. Preheat the oven to 375°F. Line a baking sheet with parchment paper and place the chicken and bell peppers on top.
2. In a small bowl, mix the seasoning blend, basil, lemon juice, and oil. Coat all the pieces evenly with the seasoning mixture on the baking sheet.
3. Bake for 20 minutes, until the chicken is slightly golden and cooked through, and the bell peppers are fork-tender. Divide into even portions and serve. Alternatively, this dish may be stored in the refrigerator in an airtight container for up to 3 days.

Nutrition Info:
- Per Serving: Calories: 185 ; Fat: 6 g ;Cholesterol: 80 mg ;Sodium: 55 mg

Alberta Steak Salad With Roasted Baby Potatoes

Servings: 4
Cooking Time: 30 Min
Ingredients:
- 1½ pounds small new potatoes
- 2 tablespoons canola or sunflower oil, divided
- ½ teaspoon kosher salt, divided
- Freshly ground black pepper
- 1 pound beef tenderloin steaks, trimmed of visible fat
- 1 head butter lettuce, torn into pieces
- ½ cup no-salt-added canned chickpeas, rinsed and drained
- 1 baby cucumber, sliced
- 1 medium carrot, peeled and shredded or spiralized
- ½ cup Red Wine Vinaigrette
- 1 medium beet, peeled and shredded or spiralized

Directions:
1. Preheat the oven to 400°F.
2. Spread the potatoes on a rimmed baking sheet. Add 1 tablespoon of oil, ¼ teaspoon of salt, and pepper. Toss well, and slide the baking sheet into the oven; roast the potatoes for 30 minutes.
3. Meanwhile, pat the steaks dry with a paper towel, and season with the remaining ¼ teaspoon of salt and pepper. Heat the remaining 1 tablespoon of oil in an oven-safe skillet over medium-high heat. When the skillet is very hot, cook the steaks until they are browned to your liking, 2 to 3 minutes per side. (Reduce the heat if the steaks are burning.) Put the skillet with the steaks in the oven, and roast to your desired level of doneness, 7 to 10 minutes. (A meat thermometer should read between 120°F for rare to 145°F for medium-well done. The temperature will continue to rise while the meat rests.)
4. While the meat and potatoes are cooking, combine the lettuce, chickpeas, cucumber, and carrot in a large bowl.
5. When the steak is ready, transfer it to a cutting board and tent with aluminum foil. Let it rest for at least 5 minutes before slicing against the grain.
6. Toss the salad with the vinaigrette, and top with the steak and beets. Serve the potatoes on the side.

Nutrition Info:
- Per Serving: Calories: 536; Fat: 28 g ;Cholesterol: 69 mg ;Sodium: 474 mg

Oat Risotto With Mushrooms, Kale, And Chicken

Servings: 4
Cooking Time: 30 Min
Ingredients:
- 4 cups reduced-sodium chicken broth
- 1 tablespoon extra-virgin olive oil
- 1 small onion, finely chopped
- 1 pound sliced mushrooms
- 1 pound boneless, skinless chicken thighs, cut into bite-size pieces
- 1¼ cups quick-cooking steel-cut oats
- 1 (10-ounce) package frozen chopped kale (about 4 cups)
- ½ cup grated Parmesan cheese (optional)
- Freshly ground black pepper (optional)

Directions:
1. In a medium saucepan, bring the broth to a simmer over medium-low heat.
2. Warm the olive oil in a large, nonstick skillet over medium-high heat. Sauté the onion and mushrooms until the onion is translucent, about 5 minutes. Push the vegetables to the side, and add the chicken. Let it sit untouched until it browns, about 2 minutes.

3. Add the oats. Cook for 1 minute, stirring constantly. Add ½ cup of the hot broth, and stir until it is completely absorbed. Continue stirring in broth, ½ cup at a time, until it is absorbed and the oats and chicken are cooked, about 10 minutes. If you run out of broth, switch to hot water.
4. Stir in the frozen kale, and cook until it's warm. Top with Parmesan and black pepper, if you like.

Nutrition Info:
- Per Serving: Calories: 470 ; Fat: 16 g ;Cholesterol: 118 mg ;Sodium: 389 mg

Lamb Goulash

Servings: 4
Cooking Time: 50 Min
Ingredients:
- 2 tbsp olive oil
- 1 lb. boneless lamb shoulder, diced
- 1 large brown onion, finely chopped
- 2 large carrots, peeled and chopped
- 1 (15 oz) can garbanzo beans, drained and rinsed
- 1 tsp paprika
- 1 tsp ground coriander
- ½ tsp ground ginger
- 4 cups water
- Fine sea salt
- Ground black pepper

Directions:
1. Heat the olive oil in a large stockpot over high heat.
2. Add the diced lamb, and brown for 3 to 5 minutes per side. Leave the juices in the pot, and transfer the lamb onto a plate.
3. Add the chopped onion and chopped carrots to the pot, and cook for 3 to 5 minutes, or until softened.
4. Add the garbanzo beans, paprika, ground coriander and ground ginger, and mix to combine.
5. Transfer the lamb back into the pot, along with the juices that collected on the plate. Add the water, and allow to boil.
6. Reduce the heat to low, cover, and allow to simmer for 30 to 40 minutes, or until the lamb is tender. Remove from the heat, and season with fine sea salt and ground black pepper to taste. Serve immediately.

Nutrition Info:
- Per Serving: Calories: 399 ; Fat: 25 g ;Cholesterol:0 mg ;Sodium: 501 mg

Tangy Italian Beef Sandwiches

Servings: 8
Cooking Time: 8 Hours
Ingredients:
- 4 pounds eye of round boneless roast, trimmed of fat
- 1 (16-ounce) jar pepperoncini, with all but ¼ cup of their liquid
- 8 French sub buns, sliced

Directions:
1. Place the beef roast in a 6-quart slow cooker. Top it with the pepperoncini and the liquid. Cover and cook on low for 8 hours.
2. Shred the meat using two forks and return it to the slow cooker.
3. Drizzle some of the accumulated juices over the inside portion of the bun before filling with the shredded beef. Serve immediately.

Nutrition Info:
- Per Serving: Calories: 463 ; Fat: 10 g;Cholesterol: 109 mg ;Sodium: 425 mg

Tomato Chicken Bake

Servings: 4
Cooking Time: 30 Min
Ingredients:
- 2 tbsp avocado oil
- 4 bone-in chicken thighs, skins removed
- ¾ tsp fine sea salt, divided
- ½ tsp ground black pepper, divided
- 1 (15 oz) can low-sodium diced tomatoes, drained
- ¼ cup water
- 1 (15 oz) can asparagus, drained
- ¼ cup black olives, pitted
- ¼ cup cilantro, chopped

Directions:
1. Heat the oven to 350ºF, gas mark 4.
2. In a large, cast iron or oven safe pan, heat the avocado oil over medium-high heat.
3. Season the chicken thighs with ¼ tsp of fine sea salt and ¼ tsp of ground black pepper. Place the chicken into the pan, and cook for 2 to 3 minutes per side, or until browned. Transfer to a plate.
4. Mix the diced tomatoes and water in the pan, and deglaze by scraping the bottom.
5. Add the asparagus, pitted olives, ½ tsp fine sea salt, and ¼ tsp ground black pepper. Mix to combine.
6. Transfer the chicken thighs back into the pan, and turn the heat off.
7. Place the oven proof pan into the oven, and bake for 20 minutes, or until the chicken is fully cooked. Remove from the oven, sprinkle with chopped cilantro, and serve hot.

Nutrition Info:
- Per Serving: Calories: 270 ; Fat: 13 g ;Cholesterol: 0 mg ;Sodium:514 mg

Sliced Pork Loin For Sandwiches

Servings: 4
Cooking Time: 30 Min
Ingredients:
- 1 teaspoon onion powder
- ½ teaspoon garlic powder
- ½ teaspoon dried thyme
- ¼ teaspoon kosher salt
- ¼ teaspoon freshly ground black pepper
- 1 (1-pound) boneless pork tenderloin roast
- 1 tablespoon canola or sunflower oil

Directions:
1. Preheat the oven to 425°F.
2. Mix the onion powder, garlic powder, thyme, salt, and pepper in a small bowl. Trim the tenderloin of any silverskin, and pat dry. Rub all over with the seasoning.
3. Heat the oil in a large, oven-safe skillet over medium-high heat. (If you don't have an oven-safe skillet, use a regular skillet and place an aluminum foil–lined roasting pan in the oven to heat up.) When the skillet is very hot, sear the pork for 2 minutes on each side. Transfer the skillet to the oven (or transfer the steak to the roasting pan).
4. Cook until the internal temperature reaches 145°F, about 15 minutes. Tent lightly with foil for at least 5 minutes before slicing.

Nutrition Info:
- Per Serving: Calories: 158 ; Fat: 6 g ;Cholesterol: 74 mg ;Sodium: 181 mg

Flank Steak And Hummus Salad

Servings: 4
Cooking Time: 15 Minutes
Ingredients:
- 1 pound flank steak
- Salt
- Freshly ground black pepper
- 8 cups chopped romaine lettuce
- ½ English cucumber, chopped
- ½ cup Yogurt-Herb Dressing, divided
- ½ cup Garlic Hummus

Directions:
1. Preheat the broiler on high.
2. Season the steak with salt and pepper. Put the steak on a baking sheet.
3. Transfer the baking sheet to the oven, and broil for 5 to 6 minutes. Flip the steak, and broil for 4 to 7 more minutes, depending on your desired doneness. Remove from the oven. Let rest for 10 minutes, then thinly slice against the grain.
4. In a large bowl, toss together the lettuce and cucumber.
5. Drizzle with half of the dressing, and toss again.
6. Serve the salad topped with the steak and hummus.
7. Drizzle with the remaining dressing if desired.

Nutrition Info:
- Per Serving: Calories: 271 ; Fat: 12g ;Cholesterol: 0mg ;Sodium: 256 mg

Garlic-Balsamic Beef Skewers

Servings: 3
Cooking Time: 2 Minutes

Ingredients:
- FOR THE MARINADE
- ½ cup aged balsamic vinegar
- 2 tablespoons low-sodium Worcestershire sauce
- 1 teaspoon garlic powder
- 1 pound sirloin steak, cut into 1-inch cubes
- FOR THE SKEWERS
- 1 tablespoon olive oil
- 1 cup low-sodium chicken broth
- 2 large red bell peppers, chopped into 1-inch pieces
- 2 cups sliced mushrooms
- 1 medium zucchini, sliced
- ½ teaspoon garlic powder

Directions:
1. TO MAKE THE MARINADE
2. In a medium bowl, combine the vinegar, Worcestershire, and garlic powder, then portion out half into an airtight container; set the remainder aside. Add the steak cubes to the container, mix well, cover, and marinate for 1 hour.
3. TO MAKE THE SKEWERS
4. Select Sauté and wait 30 seconds for the Instant Pot to warm. Pour in the oil and heat for 30 seconds, until it starts to sizzle. Add the steak cubes with the marinade, then cook for 3 minutes. Gently flip to another side and sauté for 1 minute more (it's okay if there's still some pink color to the meat).
5. Add the broth to the pot so that it covers the meat by three-quarters. Place the trivet on top. Place the peppers, mushrooms, and zucchini in a 6-inch round cake pan and set it on top of the trivet.
6. Lock the lid into place. Select Pressure Cook and cook on high pressure for 2 minutes. When the cooking is complete, allow the pressure to release naturally for 5 minutes, then quick release any remaining pressure and remove the lid.
7. Remove all the ingredients from the Instant Pot. Skewer the veggies and beef, alternating between them, and transfer to a large plate.
8. Drizzle the reserved marinade over the skewers and dust with garlic powder. Serve immediately.

Nutrition Info:
- Per Serving: Calories: 355 ; Fat: 8 g ;Cholesterol: 92 mg ;Sodium: 174 mg

Chapter 4 Fish And Seafood Mains Recipes

Pine Nut Haddock

Servings: 2
Cooking Time: 15 Min
Ingredients:
- Aluminum foil
- ½ cup cilantro, roughly chopped
- ¼ cup pine nuts
- ¼ tsp ground cumin
- ¼ tsp ground black pepper
- 2 tsp olive oil
- 1 large orange, zested and cut in half
- 2 (4 oz) haddock fillets, skin removed

Directions:
1. Heat the oven to 375°F, gas mark 5. Line a baking sheet with aluminum foil.
2. In a food processor, combine the cilantro, pine nuts, ground cumin, ground black pepper, olive oil, and orange zest, and pulse until fine and incorporated.
3. Cut one half of the orange into 4 slices. Place 2 orange slices on the baking sheet, overlapping each other, then place the haddock fillet on top. Repeat with the remaining orange slices and fish fillet.
4. Spread 1½ tbsp of the pine nut mixture on top of each haddock fillet. Squeeze the juice from the other half of the orange on top.
5. Bake for 10 to 12 minutes, until the haddock fillets flake easily with a fork. Serve warm.

Nutrition Info:
- Per Serving: Calories: 294 ; Fat: 21 g ;Cholesterol: 56 mg ;Sodium: 40 mg

Citrus Tilapia

Servings: 2
Cooking Time: 25 Min
Ingredients:
- Aluminum foil
- 2 tbsp garlic, minced
- 2 rosemary sprigs, stems removed, chopped
- 1 oregano sprig, stem removed, chopped
- 2 tbsp olive oil
- 2 tilapia filets, cleaned and rinsed
- 2 lemons, sliced and divided
- 2 limes, sliced and divided
- ¼ tsp fine sea salt
- ¼ tsp ground black pepper

Directions:
1. Heat the oven to 450ºF, gas mark 8. Line a baking sheet with aluminum foil.
2. In a medium-sized mixing bowl, add together the minced garlic, chopped rosemary, chopped oregano, and olive oil. Mix to combine.
3. Add the tilapia fillets to the bowl, and coat generously with the olive oil mixture. Place the fillets on the prepared baking sheet.
4. Place half the lemon and lime slices on the fillets, and season with fine sea salt and ground black pepper.
5. Place the baking sheet in the oven, and bake for 18 to 22 minutes, or until the fillets are cooked through. Remove from the oven.
6. Serve with your choice of side, and garnish with the remaining lemon and lime slices.

Nutrition Info:
- Per Serving: Calories: 218 ; Fat: 3 g ;Cholesterol: 0mg ;Sodium: 430 mg

Fish Florentine

Servings: 2
Cooking Time: 10 Minutes
Ingredients:
- 2 teaspoons avocado oil, divided
- 2 garlic cloves, minced
- 1 red bell pepper, diced
- 1 (6-ounce) bag fresh spinach (about 4 cups)
- ¼ cup Cashew Cream Dressing
- 2 (4-ounce) rainbow trout fillets, skinned and thoroughly patted dry
- ¼ teaspoon freshly ground black pepper

Directions:
1. In a medium skillet, heat 1 teaspoon of oil over medium heat. Add the garlic and bell pepper and simmer for about 2 minutes, until the mixture becomes fragrant and sizzles lightly.
2. Add the spinach and stir occasionally, until wilted, about 2 minutes.
3. Remove from the heat and add the dressing.
4. In another medium skillet, heat the remaining 1 teaspoon of oil over medium heat. Heat for 2 minutes. Add the fillets and season with pepper. Cook for 2 minutes and when the middle puffs up and the spatula can easily lift the fish, flip them and cook for another 2 minutes. (Cook the fish lightly. Do not overdo it. Timing is critical.)
5. On two plates, divide the spinach mixture evenly so that it encompasses the fish fillets on top and bottom, then serve.

Nutrition Info:
- Per Serving: Calories: 402 ; Fat: 26 g ;Cholesterol: 56 mg;Sodium: 97 mg

Lemon & Lime Tuna

Servings: 2
Cooking Time: 15 Min
Ingredients:
- 2 tsp plant-based butter
- 2 slices whole-grain bread
- 1 (5 oz) can water packed tuna, drained
- 2 tsp olive oil
- 2 tsp lite mayonnaise
- 1 tsp lemon zest
- 1 tsp lime zest
- 1 tbsp lemon juice
- 1 tbsp lime juice
- 2 tbsp red onion, finely chopped
- ½ tsp paprika (optional)
- Ground black pepper
- ¼ cup cheese blend, shredded

Directions:
1. Preheat the broiler, and set the oven rack about 6 inches from the heat.
2. Spread plant butter thinly on both sides of the whole-grain bread slices, and place them on a baking sheet.
3. Toast the bread under the broiler for 2 minutes on each side, until it is golden brown. Make sure it doesn't burn.
4. In a medium-sized mixing bowl, combine the drained tuna, olive oil, lite mayonnaise, lemon zest, lime zest, lemon juice, lime juice, chopped red onion, paprika (if using), and ground black pepper. Mix until fully incorporated.
5. Divide the tuna mixture between the two slices of toasted bread, and sprinkle with the shredded cheese blend.
6. Broil for 2 to 3 minutes, until the cheese has melted.

Nutrition Info:
- Per Serving: Calories: 336 ; Fat: 19 g ;Cholesterol: 46 mg ;Sodium: 450 mg

Poached Fish In Tomato-Caper Sauce

Servings: 4
Cooking Time: 30 Minutes
Ingredients:
- 1 (28-ounce) can low-sodium diced tomatoes
- ¼ cup capers, drained, rinsed, and finely chopped
- 3 garlic cloves, minced
- 1 teaspoon paprika
- ½ teaspoon salt
- ¼ teaspoon freshly ground black pepper
- 1 pound cod or halibut fillets

Directions:
1. In a large saucepan, combine the tomatoes with their juices, capers, garlic, paprika, salt, and pepper. Bring to a simmer over medium heat. Cook, stirring occasionally, for 15 minutes, or until thickened.
2. Using a spatula, slide the fillets into the saucepan, and cook for 10 to 15 minutes, or until they flake easily with a fork. Remove from the heat.

Nutrition Info:
- Per Serving: Calories: 130 ; Fat: 1 g ;Cholesterol:0mg ;Sodium: 338 mg

Pistachio Flounder Fillets

Servings: 4
Cooking Time: 30 Min
Ingredients:
- Aluminum foil
- 2 tbsp avocado oil, divided
- 1 medium cabbage head, halved stem removed
- ½ tbsp garlic, crushed
- ½ cup all-purpose flour
- 1 large free-range egg, beaten
- 2 tbsp water
- ¼ tsp paprika
- ½ cup unsalted pistachios, finely chopped
- 12 oz flounder fillets, fresh or thawed
- ¼ tsp fine sea salt
- Ground black pepper
- 1 lime, cut into wedges

Directions:
1. Heat the oven to 425°F, gas mark 7. Line two baking sheets with aluminum foil, and drizzle each with ½ tbsp of avocado oil.
2. Lay the cabbage halves, cut side up, on one sheet, and drizzle with the remaining 1 tbsp of olive oil. Sprinkle the cabbage with the crushed garlic.
3. Set the second baking sheet next to three medium-sized mixing bowls. Fill one mixing bowl with the all-purpose flour. Fill another with the beaten egg, water, and paprika - mix to combine. In the third mixing bowl, place the finely chopped pistachios.
4. Pat the flounder fillets dry with a paper towel. Season with fine sea salt and ground black pepper.
5. Dip and flip each flounder fillet in the all-purpose flour, then the beaten egg mixture, then the chopped pistachios. Lay the fillets on the baking sheet, and press any loose pistachios into the flounder.
6. Place both baking sheets in the oven, and roast for 8 to 10 minutes, or until the fish starts to flake easily with a fork.
7. At this point, the cabbage should be nicely browned. If not, remove the flounder fillets from the oven, and broil the cabbage for 2 to 3 minutes, watching carefully. Serve with lime wedges.

Nutrition Info:
- Per Serving: Calories: 367 ; Fat: 21 g ;Cholesterol: 96 mg ;Sodium: 80 mg

Broiled Pesto Cod

Servings: 4
Cooking Time: 25 Minutes
Ingredients:
- 1 pound cod fillets
- Salt
- Freshly ground black pepper
- ¼ cup Basil-Walnut Pesto
- 2 tablespoons whole-wheat panko bread crumbs
- 1 large tomato, chopped

Directions:
1. Preheat the oven to 400°F. Line a baking sheet with parchment paper.
2. Put the cod on the prepared baking sheet. Season lightly with salt and pepper.
3. Spread the pesto over the cod in an even layer.
4. Sprinkle the bread crumbs on top.
5. Transfer the baking sheet to the oven, and bake for 16 to 20 minutes, or until the bread crumbs have browned and the cod flakes easily with a fork. Remove from the oven, leaving the oven on.
6. Top the cod with the tomato.
7. Return the baking sheet to the oven, and bake for 2 minutes, or until the tomato is heated through. Remove from the oven.

Nutrition Info:
- Per Serving: Calories: 183 ; Fat: 9 g ;Cholesterol:0mg ;Sodium: 549 mg

Spicy Herring Pasta

Servings: 2
Cooking Time: 15 Min
Ingredients:
- 2 tsp olive oil
- 1 medium red onion, diced
- 1 tbsp garlic, minced
- 1 lb. beefsteak tomatoes, cut into pieces
- 1 (3 oz) can boneless herring in water
- ¼ cup low-sodium capers
- ½ tsp dried rosemary
- ½ cup cilantro, chopped
- ¼ tsp red pepper flakes

- ¼ tsp paprika
- ¼ tsp cayenne pepper
- ½ tsp ground black pepper

Directions:

1. Heat the olive oil in a medium-sized frying pan over medium-high heat. Add the diced onions and minced garlic, and fry for 2 minutes, or until translucent.
2. Add the tomato pieces, and cook covered for 5 minutes, until the tomatoes have softened.
3. Drain the herring fillets, and place in a small mixing bowl. Mash well with a fork.
4. Add the mashed herring fillets, capers, dried rosemary, chopped cilantro, red pepper flakes, paprika, cayenne pepper, and ground black pepper to the tomato mixture. Mix to combine.
5. Cook on low heat, covered, for 5 minutes, or until heated through.
6. Serve ½ of the herring mixture on a pasta of your choice for each person. Serve warm.

Nutrition Info:

- Per Serving: Calories: 278 ; Fat: 15g ;Cholesterol:51 mg ;Sodium: 241 mg

Rainbow Trout Fillets With Parsley, Pecan, And Oranges

Servings: 2
Cooking Time: 15 Minutes
Ingredients:

- ½ cup chopped fresh parsley (about ¼ bunch)
- ¼ cup unsalted pecans
- ¼ teaspoon ground cumin
- ¼ teaspoon freshly ground black pepper
- 2 teaspoons avocado oil
- 1 large navel orange, divided
- 2 (4-ounce) rainbow trout fillets, skin removed

Directions:

1. Preheat the oven to 375°F. Line a baking sheet with parchment paper.
2. In a blender, pulse the parsley, pecans, cumin, pepper, and oil.
3. Zest the outside of the orange then slice the orange in half. Add the zest to the parsley-pecan mixture.
4. Cut one half of the orange into 2 slices. Put 2 orange slices on the baking sheet, overlapping each other, then place the fillet on top. Repeat with the remaining orange half and fillet.
5. Place half the parsley-pecan mixture on top of each fillet (about 1½ tablespoons each). Squeeze the other half of the orange on top.
6. Bake for 10 to 12 minutes, until the rainbow trout turns white and flaky, then serve.

Nutrition Info:

- Per Serving: Calories: 294 ; Fat: 21 g ;Cholesterol: 56 mg;Sodium: 40 mg

Pistachio-Crusted Halibut

Servings: 2
Cooking Time: 15 Minutes
Ingredients:

- 1 tablespoon Dijon mustard
- 1 teaspoon pure maple syrup
- 1 teaspoon avocado oil
- 2 garlic cloves, minced
- ½ teaspoon freshly ground black pepper
- 2 (4-ounce) halibut fillets, skin on, scaled
- 2 tablespoons unsalted pistachios

Directions:

1. Preheat the oven to 425°F. Line a baking sheet with parchment paper.
2. In a medium mixing bowl, combine the mustard, maple syrup, oil, garlic, and pepper. Coat the halibut fillets evenly with the mixture and place them on the prepared baking sheet.
3. Top each fillet with 1 tablespoon of pistachios and cook for 12 to 15 minutes, until the pistachios are lightly browned and the fish is opaque and flaky, then serve.

Nutrition Info:

- Per Serving: Calories: 208 ; Fat: 10 g ;Cholesterol: 82 mg;Sodium: 215 mg

Sofrito Cod Stew

Servings: 4
Cooking Time: 30 Min
Ingredients:
- 1 cup uncooked parboiled brown rice
- ¼ cup extra-virgin olive oil
- 1 large onion, finely chopped
- 1 green bell pepper, seeded and finely chopped
- 5 garlic cloves, minced
- 1 (28-ounce) can no-salt-added whole tomatoes
- 1 teaspoon dried thyme
- ¼ teaspoon salt
- ¼ teaspoon freshly ground black pepper
- 1 pound sustainably sourced cod fillets, fresh or thawed
- ½ teaspoon red pepper flakes (optional)

Directions:
1. Cook the rice according to the package directions.
2. Meanwhile, heat the olive oil in a large skillet over medium heat. Add the onion, bell pepper, and garlic, and cook until softened, 5 to 7 minutes.
3. Turn up the heat, and add the tomatoes with their juice, thyme, salt, and black pepper. When it starts to boil, add the cod, pushing it down into the liquid, and turn down the heat so it simmers gently for 7 to 8 minutes.
4. Test the fish by flaking with a fork. If it flakes easily, separate it into bite-size pieces. If not, cook for a few more minutes.
5. Taste and adjust the seasonings, adding red pepper flakes if desired. Serve over the rice.

Nutrition Info:
- Per Serving: Calories: 449 ; Fat: 16 g ;Cholesterol:492 mg ;Sodium: 233 mg

Salmon Over Lentils

Servings: 4
Cooking Time: 25 Minutes
Ingredients:
- 1 cup dried brown lentils
- 4 (4-ounce) salmon fillets
- ½ teaspoon salt, divided
- ¼ teaspoon freshly ground black pepper
- 2 tablespoons extra-virgin olive oil
- 1 onion, chopped
- 1 carrot, finely chopped
- 1 teaspoon dried thyme

Directions:
1. Preheat the oven to 400°F. Line a baking sheet with parchment paper.
2. In a large saucepan, cover the lentils with water by about 2 inches. Bring to a boil.
3. Reduce the heat to low. Simmer for 20 minutes, or until the lentils are just tender but not mushy. Remove from the heat. Drain.
4. While the lentils are cooking, put the salmon on the prepared baking sheet. Season with ¼ teaspoon of salt and the pepper.
5. Transfer the baking sheet to the oven, and bake for 15 to 20 minutes, or until the salmon flakes easily with a fork. Remove from the oven.
6. In a skillet, heat the oil over medium-high heat.
7. Add the onion and carrot. Sauté for 3 to 5 minutes, or until just softened.
8. Add the thyme and remaining ¼ teaspoon of salt.
9. Stir in the lentils, and mix well. Remove from the heat.
10. Serve the salmon fillets on a bed of lentils.

Nutrition Info:
- Per Serving: Calories: 407 ; Fat: 15 g ;Cholesterol:0mg ;Sodium: 355 mg

Mustard-Dill Salmon With Lemon And Asparagus

Servings: 2
Cooking Time: 15 Minutes
Ingredients:
- 10 asparagus spears, trimmed 1 inch from bottom
- ¼ teaspoon freshly ground black pepper
- 1 lemon, divided
- 2 (4-ounce) salmon fillets, skin removed
- 2 tablespoons stone-ground mustard
- ¼ cup chopped fresh dill

Directions:

1. Preheat the oven to 375°F. Line a baking sheet with parchment paper.
2. Put the asparagus on the prepared baking sheet and season with pepper. Divide the asparagus into sections, five for each fish.
3. Cut the lemon in half. Reserve one half for squeezing after the fish is cooked and slice the other half into ¼-inch-thick slices.
4. Place the lemon slices in the middle of the asparagus and then place the fish on top of the lemons.
5. In a small mixing bowl, combine the mustard and dill. Divide and evenly spread half the mixture on top of each fish.
6. Cook for about 15 minutes until the fish becomes opaque and flakes easily.
7. Squeeze the lemon juice from the reserved lemon half on both fillets and enjoy.

Nutrition Info:
- Per Serving: Calories: 171 ; Fat: 5 g ;Cholesterol: 55 mg;Sodium: 76 mg

Mahi Mahi With Leeks, Ginger, And Baby Bok Choy

Servings: 2
Cooking Time: 15 Minutes
Ingredients:
- 2 teaspoons toasted sesame oil
- 1 whole leek (including green top), diced (about 2 cups)
- 1 packed tablespoon grated ginger
- 3 bunches baby bok choy, separated
- 2 (4-ounce) mahi mahi fillets, skinned
- ¼ teaspoon freshly ground black pepper
- ¼ teaspoon garlic powder

Directions:
1. Heat a 5-quart pot over medium heat, pour in the sesame oil, and add the leek. Sauté until fragrant and translucent, 1 to 2 minutes.
2. Add the ginger and bok choy, stir to combine, and cover for 5 minutes, until the dish is fragrant and the bok choy is fork-tender but not soft.
3. In the pot, move the bok choy to the side and add the mahi mahi fillets so that they touch the surface of the pot. Season the fillets with the pepper and garlic powder and cook for 3 minutes, until the skin and ¼ inch from the bottom turns white.
4. Flip the mahi mahi and add the leek, ginger, and bok choy mixture on top. Cook for another 2 to 3 minutes until the mahi mahi is cooked, flaky, and tender. Serve.

Nutrition Info:
- Per Serving: Calories: 193 ; Fat: 6 g ;Cholesterol: 80 mg;Sodium: 192 mg

Pan-Seared Salmon With Chimichurri Sauce

Servings: 2
Cooking Time: 10 Minutes
Ingredients:
- 2 teaspoons avocado oil
- 2 (4-ounce) salmon fillets, skin intact but scaled
- ½ teaspoon Mediterranean Seasoning Rub Blend
- 1 tablespoon Chimichurri Sauce

Directions:
1. In a medium skillet, heat the oil over medium heat for 3 minutes, until very hot.
2. Add the fish skin-side down to the pan. You should hear a sizzling noise or else the pan is not hot enough. Season each flesh side of the fish with ¼ teaspoon of the seasoning blend.
3. Cook for another 3 minutes until ¼ inch of the bottom of the fish is opaque and the fish is easily flipped with a spatula. If it sticks to the pan, it may need a little more time.
4. Flip and cook the flesh side for 2 to 3 minutes, until the whole fish is opaque and cooked through.
5. Plate the salmon, add ½ tablespoon of the sauce to each piece, and serve.

Nutrition Info:
- Per Serving: Calories: 202 ; Fat: 12 g ;Cholesterol: 64 mg;Sodium: 147 mg

Shrimp Paella

Servings: 4
Cooking Time: 40 Minutes
Ingredients:
- 2 tablespoons extra-virgin olive oil, divided
- 1 pound large shrimp, peeled and deveined
- 1 onion, chopped
- 2 cups medium-grain white rice
- 3½ cups water
- 1 (14½-ounce) can low-sodium diced tomatoes, drained
- ½ teaspoon paprika
- ¼ teaspoon salt
- ¼ teaspoon freshly ground black pepper

Directions:
1. In a large skillet, heat 1 tablespoon of oil over medium-high heat.
2. Add the shrimp, and cook for 2 to 3 minutes per side, or until just cooked through, being careful not to overcook. Transfer to a plate.
3. In the same skillet, heat the remaining 1 tablespoon of oil over medium heat.
4. Add the onion, and cook for 3 to 5 minutes, or until softened.
5. Add the rice, and stir to coat with the oil.
6. Add the water, tomatoes, paprika, salt, and pepper. Bring to a boil.
7. Reduce the heat to a simmer. Cover the skillet, and cook for 20 to 25 minutes, or until the water has been absorbed. Remove from the heat.
8. Stir in the shrimp.

Nutrition Info:
- Per Serving: Calories: 519; Fat: 9 g ;Cholesterol:0mg ;Sodium: 334 mg

Tomato And Zucchini With Salmon And Farro

Servings: 4
Cooking Time: 25 Min
Ingredients:
- 1 cup uncooked farro
- 2 tablespoons extra-virgin olive oil
- 4 shallots, thinly sliced
- 2 cups cherry tomatoes, halved
- 1 teaspoon dried thyme
- 1 medium zucchini
- 2 garlic cloves
- Zest and juice of 1 lemon (about 3 tablespoons juice)
- 1 (7.5-ounce) can wild salmon, drained
- 4 cups baby spinach
- ½ cup crumbled feta cheese

Directions:
1. Cook the farro according to the package directions.
2. Meanwhile, heat the oil in a large skillet over medium heat. Add the shallots, tomatoes, and thyme. Cook until the shallots start to brown, 5 or 6 minutes.
3. While that's cooking, grate or spiralize the zucchini and mince the garlic.
4. Add the zucchini, garlic, and lemon zest and juice to the skillet with the tomatoes, and cook for a few minutes, stirring occasionally.
5. Drain the salmon, reserving 1 tablespoon of the liquid from the can. Add the salmon to the skillet, along with the reserved canning liquid. Break the fish apart with a fork. Add the cooked farro and the spinach. Stir everything together to heat through.
6. Taste and adjust the seasonings. Top with the feta cheese.

Nutrition Info:
- Per Serving: Calories: 405 ; Fat: 15 g ;Cholesterol: 52 mg ;Sodium: 411 mg

Mediterranean Mahi-Mahi

Servings: 4
Cooking Time: 20 Min
Ingredients:
- 8 oz uncooked egg noodles
- 5 cups cauliflower florets
- 2 tbsp olive oil, divided
- 1 lb. Mahi-Mahi fillets, fresh, or frozen and thawed
- ¼ tsp fine sea salt
- Ground black pepper
- 1 tsp Italian seasoning
- 10 black olives, pitted and sliced

- 1 lemon, zested and juiced

Directions:
1. Heat the oven to 450°F, gas mark 8.
2. Fill a large stockpot with water, and allow to boil over high heat. Cook the egg noodles until al dente, or follow the package instructions. In the final 2 to 3 minutes of cooking the noodles, add the cauliflower florets.
3. Lay the Mahi-Mahi fillets on a baking sheet, and brush with 1 tbsp of olive oil. Sprinkle with fine sea salt and ground black pepper.
4. Bake the Mahi-Mahi fillets for 12 minutes, or until easily flaked with a fork.
5. Drain the pasta and veggies in a colander, and transfer to a large serving bowl. Add the remaining 1 tbsp olive oil, Italian seasoning, sliced olives, and lemon zest and juice.
6. Use a fork to flake the baked Mahi-Mahi into the pasta. Mix to combine, and serve warm.

Nutrition Info:
- Per Serving: Calories: 462 ; Fat: 15 g ;Cholesterol: 100 mg ;Sodium: 419 mg

Lemon-Rosemary Salmon

Servings: 4
Cooking Time: 20 Minutes
Ingredients:
- Zest and juice of ½ lemon
- 1 tablespoon extra-virgin olive oil
- 2 teaspoons whole-grain mustard
- ½ teaspoon dried rosemary
- ¼ teaspoon salt
- ¼ teaspoon freshly ground black pepper
- 1 pound salmon fillets

Directions:
1. Preheat the oven to 400°F. Line a baking sheet with parchment paper.
2. In a small bowl, combine the lemon zest and juice, oil, mustard, rosemary, salt, and pepper.
3. Put the salmon on the prepared baking sheet.
4. Spread the mixture on the salmon.
5. Transfer the baking sheet to the oven, and bake for 16 to 20 minutes, or until the salmon has cooked through and flakes easily with a fork. Remove from the oven.

Nutrition Info:
- Per Serving: Calories:194 ; Fat: 11 g ;Cholesterol:0mg ;Sodium: 223 mg

Mussels With White Wine Sauce

Servings: 4
Cooking Time: 15 Minutes
Ingredients:
- 2 pounds mussels
- ½ cup dry white wine
- 2 tablespoons extra-virgin olive oil
- 3 garlic cloves, minced
- ¼ cup chopped fresh parsley

Directions:
1. Clean and prep the mussels. Remove any beards.
2. Put the mussels and wine in a large pot. Bring to a boil.
3. Cover the pot, and reduce the heat to low. The mussels will release juices as they cook. Cook for 5 to 7 minutes, or until the mussels have opened. Remove from the heat. Using a slotted spoon, remove the mussels from the pot, leaving the liquid in the pot. Discard any mussels that have not opened.
4. Let the liquid rest for a couple of minutes, then carefully pour the liquid off the top into a small bowl, leaving behind the grit and sediment.
5. In a small saucepan, heat the oil over medium heat.
6. Add the garlic, and sauté for 30 seconds, or until fragrant.
7. Add the cooking liquid, and simmer for 2 to 3 minutes, or until slightly reduced. Remove from the heat.
8. Serve the mussels with the sauce poured over them.
9. Garnish with the parsley.

Nutrition Info:
- Per Serving: Calories: 137 ; Fat: 8 g ;Cholesterol:0mg ;Sodium: 166 mg

Tuna, Cashew, And Couscous Salad

Servings: 3
Cooking Time: 15 Min
Ingredients:
- ½ cup uncooked whole-wheat couscous
- ¼ teaspoon salt
- 1 (5-ounce) can sustainably sourced tuna, packed in oil
- 1 bell pepper, any color, seeded and chopped
- 1 (12-ounce) package broccoli slaw (about 4 cups)
- 3 scallions, finely chopped
- 3 tablespoons red wine vinegar
- 2 tablespoons extra-virgin olive oil
- 1 teaspoon dried oregano
- 1 teaspoon dried thyme
- ½ teaspoon freshly ground black pepper
- ½ cup chopped unsalted roasted cashews

Directions:
1. Prepare the couscous with the salt, according to the package directions. Transfer to a medium bowl, and let it cool until the other ingredients are ready.
2. Drain the tuna, and use a fork to mash it well in a large bowl. Add the bell pepper, broccoli slaw, scallions, vinegar, oil, oregano, thyme, and black pepper.
3. Add the couscous, and toss well. Adjust the seasonings, if desired. Top with the cashews.

Nutrition Info:
- Per Serving: Calories: 457 ; Fat: 24g ;Cholesterol: 15 mg ;Sodium: 450 mg

Creamy Tuna Salad

Servings: 2
Cooking Time: 10 Min
Ingredients:
- 1 (5 oz) can water-packed tuna, drained
- 1 large, ripe avocado, pitted, peeled, and mashed
- 2 spring onions, finely chopped
- ½ lime, juiced
- 2 tbsp avocado oil
- ¼ tsp fine sea salt
- ¼ tsp ground black pepper
- 4 whole-wheat bread slices

Directions:
1. In a small mixing bowl, add together the drained tuna, mashed avocado, chopped spring onion, lime juice, avocado oil, fine sea salt and ground black pepper. Mix until well combined.
2. Spoon the avocado mixture equally between 2 slices of bread, and top with the remaining two slices. Serve cold.

Nutrition Info:
- Per Serving: Calories: 518 ; Fat: 32 g ;Cholesterol:0mg ;Sodium: 567mg

Pan-Seared Halibut With Chimichurri

Servings: 4
Cooking Time: 10 Min
Ingredients:
- 2 tablespoons extra-virgin olive oil
- 4 (5- to 6-ounce) sustainably sourced halibut fillets, fresh or thawed
- 1 recipe Chimichurri

Directions:
1. Heat the oil in a large, nonstick skillet over medium-high heat. When the oil is hot, sear the halibut for about 5 minutes on each side, until it flakes easily and is cooked to an internal temperature of 145°F.
2. Serve immediately, topped with the Chimichurri.

Nutrition Info:
- Per Serving: Calories: 371 ; Fat: 25 g ;Cholesterol: 112 mg ;Sodium: 248 mg

Sheet Pan Tahini Cod With Broccoli

Servings: 2
Cooking Time: 20 Minutes
Ingredients:
- 2 (4-ounce) cod fillets, skin removed
- 2 lemons, sliced
- 2 tablespoons chopped fresh parsley
- 2 cups broccoli florets
- 4 tablespoons Tahini-Garlic Dressing, divided

Directions:
1. Preheat the oven to 400°F. Line a baking sheet with parchment paper.
2. Place the cod fillets on the prepared baking sheet and top with the lemon slices and parsley. Add the broccoli to the baking sheet and coat with 2 tablespoons of dressing.
3. Bake the cod for 10 to 12 minutes, until opaque and flaky. Leave broccoli in until it has crispy edges, about 5 minutes more.
4. To serve, divide the cod and broccoli evenly. Top the cod with the remaining 2 tablespoons of dressing and enjoy.

Nutrition Info:
- Per Serving: Calories: 258 ; Fat: 12 g ;Cholesterol: 55 mg;Sodium: 209 mg

Cod Parcels With Mushrooms And Spinach

Servings: 4
Cooking Time: 15 Minutes
Ingredients:
- 4 cups baby spinach
- 2 cups sliced shiitake mushrooms
- 4 (4-ounce) cod fillets
- ½ teaspoon Old Bay seasoning
- ½ teaspoon salt
- ¼ teaspoon freshly ground black pepper
- ¼ cup chopped scallions, green and white parts
- 2 tablespoons extra-virgin olive oil

Directions:
1. Preheat the oven to 425°F.
2. Tear 4 (12-inch) square pieces of aluminum foil. Into each piece of foil, place 1 cup of spinach and ½ cup of mushrooms.
3. Place 1 piece of cod on top.
4. Season with the Old Bay, salt, and pepper.
5. Sprinkle with the scallions, and drizzle with the oil.
6. Fold up the packets to seal and enclose the cod.
7. Place the packets on a baking sheet.
8. Transfer the baking sheet to the oven, and bake for 15 minutes. Remove from the oven. Carefully unfold the packets.

Nutrition Info:
- Per Serving: Calories: 155 ; Fat:7 g ;Cholesterol:0mg ;Sodium: 435 mg

Collard Green Halibut Wraps With Cilantro-Mint Sauce

Servings: 2
Cooking Time: 15 Minutes
Ingredients:
- 2 (4-ounce) halibut fillets, skin on, scaled
- 1 teaspoon avocado oil, divided
- ½ teaspoon Barbeque Seasoning Rub Blend, divided
- 4 collard green leaves, divided
- 4 tablespoons Cilantro-Mint Sauce

Directions:
1. Preheat the oven to 425°F. Line a baking sheet with parchment paper.
2. Place the halibut fillets skin-side down on the prepared baking sheet and season the tops and sides with oil and the barbeque seasoning.
3. Bake in the oven for 12 to 15 minutes, until the fish is opaque and flaky.
4. In the meantime, trim off the stems and cut out the thicker stems inside the leaves of the collard greens.
5. When the fish is done, add 1 tablespoon of the sauce and 2 to 3 ounces of halibut per collard green and wrap tightly. Place two wraps on each plate and serve.

Nutrition Info:
- Per Serving: Calories: 182 ; Fat: 6 g ;Cholesterol: 83 mg;Sodium: 114 mg

Shrimp Scampi

Servings: 4
Cooking Time: 10 Minutes
Ingredients:
- 2 tablespoons extra-virgin olive oil
- 6 garlic cloves, minced
- ½ cup dry white wine
- 1 pound shrimp, peeled and deveined
- ¼ teaspoon salt
- Juice of 1 lemon
- 2 tablespoons chopped fresh parsley

Directions:
1. In a large skillet, heat the oil over medium-high heat.
2. Add the garlic, and cook for 30 seconds, or until fragrant.
3. Add the wine, and simmer for 2 to 3 minutes, or until reduced by about half.
4. Add the shrimp, and cook for 3 to 5 minutes, or until cooked through and pink. Remove from the heat. Season with the salt.
5. Sprinkle the lemon juice over the shrimp.
6. Garnish with the parsley.

Nutrition Info:
- Per Serving: Calories: 190; Fat: 7 g ;Cholesterol:0mg ;Sodium: 284 mg

Walnut-And-Herb–Crusted Fish

Servings: 4
Cooking Time: 20 Minutes
Ingredients:
- ¼ cup chopped walnuts
- ¼ cup shredded Parmesan cheese
- 2 tablespoons chopped fresh parsley
- 1 tablespoon chopped fresh basil leaves
- 1 pound sole or tilapia fillets
- 2 tablespoons extra-virgin olive oil
- ¼ teaspoon salt
- ¼ teaspoon freshly ground black pepper

Directions:
1. Preheat the oven to 400°F.
2. In a food processor, combine the walnuts and cheese. Process until it forms crumbs.
3. Add the parsley and basil. Pulse until the mixture is combined.
4. Put the fillets on a baking sheet.
5. Brush the fillets with the oil. Season with the salt and pepper.
6. Press the walnut and cheese mixture into the fillets.
7. Transfer the baking sheet to the oven, and bake for 15 to 20 minutes, or until the fillets have cooked through and flake easily with a fork and the breading has browned. Remove from the oven.

Nutrition Info:
- Per Serving: Calories: 244; Fat:15 g ;Cholesterol:0mg ;Sodium: 338 mg

Sardines Puttanesca

Servings: 2
Cooking Time: 15 Minutes
Ingredients:
- 2 teaspoons avocado oil
- 1 medium yellow onion, diced
- 2 large garlic cloves, minced
- 1 pound medium Roma tomatoes, cut into ½-inch pieces
- 7½ ounces no-salt-added canned sardines, in water
- ¼ cup low-sodium Kalamata olives, quartered
- ½ teaspoon dried oregano
- ½ cup fresh chopped fresh parsley
- ¼ teaspoon red pepper flakes
- ½ teaspoon freshly ground black pepper

Directions:
1. In a medium skillet, heat the oil over medium-high heat. Add the onions and garlic and sauté until translucent, about 2 minutes.
2. Add the tomatoes and cover for 5 minutes, until the tomatoes have softened and their juices are exposed.
3. Drain the sardines and, in a small bowl, mash well with a fork.
4. Add the sardines, olives, oregano, parsley, red pepper flakes, and black pepper to the tomato, onion, and garlic mixture. Mix well and cook on medium-low heat, covered, for another 5 minutes. Serve on top of ½ cup of whole wheat

pasta or bean pasta, or alongside Whole Wheat Seed Crackers.

Nutrition Info:
- Per Serving: Calories: 278 ; Fat: 15 g ;Cholesterol: 51 mg;Sodium: 241 mg

Za'Atar Cod Fillets

Servings: 4
Cooking Time: 15 Min
Ingredients:
- Aluminum foil
- 4 (4 oz) cod fillets
- 2 tbsp olive oil
- 1 tsp za'atar
- ½ tsp fine sea salt
- ¼ tsp ground black pepper
- 1 lime, cut into wedges
- 2 tbsp cilantro, finely chopped

Directions:
1. Heat the oven to 400°F, gas mark 6. Line a baking sheet with aluminum foil.
2. Place the cod fillets on the baking sheet, and drizzle with olive oil.
3. Season both sides of the fillets with za'atar, fine sea salt, and ground black pepper.
4. Place the baking sheet in the oven, and bake for 6 to 8 minutes. Flip, and cook for 5 more minutes, or until the fillets flake easily with a fork. Remove from the oven.
5. Serve the fillets topped with the lime wedges and chopped cilantro.

Nutrition Info:
- Per Serving: Calories: 164 ; Fat: 8 g ;Cholesterol: 0mg ;Sodium: 369 mg

Electric Chickpeas And Shrimp

Servings: 3
Cooking Time: 20 Min
Ingredients:
- 7 ounces sustainably sourced, frozen cooked shrimp, thawed and peeled
- 1 (15-ounce) can no-salt-added chickpeas, rinsed and drained
- 1 red bell pepper, seeded and diced
- ⅓ cup finely chopped red onion
- 1 garlic clove, finely chopped
- ½ cup red wine vinegar
- 3 tablespoons extra-virgin olive oil
- ½ teaspoon paprika
- ½ teaspoon dried oregano
- ⅛ teaspoon salt
- Pinch cayenne pepper

Directions:
1. In a medium bowl, mash the salmon together with the mayonnaise, Sriracha, and dill. Mix in the carrot, celery, chickpeas, and sunflower seeds.
2. Spread the salmon onto 4 slices of toast. Top with the lettuce and the other slices of toast.

Nutrition Info:
- Per Serving: Calories: 338 ; Fat: 15 g ;Cholesterol: 83 mg ;Sodium: 510 mg

Weeknight Fish Skillet

Servings: 4
Cooking Time: 20 Minutes
Ingredients:
- 1 pound cod, halibut, or mahi mahi fillets
- ½ teaspoon salt
- ¼ teaspoon freshly ground black pepper
- 1 tablespoon extra-virgin olive oil
- 1 red bell pepper, cored and chopped
- 1 red onion, chopped
- 2 cups cherry tomatoes
- ¼ cup chopped pitted green olives

Directions:
1. Season the fillets with the salt and pepper.
2. In a large skillet, heat the oil over medium-high heat.
3. Add the bell pepper and onion. Cook for 3 to 5 minutes, or until softened.

4. Add the tomatoes and olives. Stir for 1 to 2 minutes, or until the tomatoes begin to soften.
5. Nestle the fillets on top of the vegetables, cover the skillet, and cook for 5 to 10 minutes, or until the fillets flake easily with a fork. Remove from the heat.

Nutrition Info:
- Per Serving: Calories: 151 ; Fat:5 g ;Cholesterol:0mg ;Sodium: 603 mg

Salmon Burgers With Dill

Servings: 4
Cooking Time: 35 Minutes
Ingredients:
- 1 pound salmon fillets
- ½ teaspoon salt, divided
- ¼ teaspoon freshly ground black pepper
- ½ cup bread crumbs
- 1 large egg
- 2 garlic cloves, minced
- ½ teaspoon dried dill
- 2 tablespoons extra-virgin olive oil

Directions:
1. Preheat the oven to 400°F. Line a baking sheet with parchment paper.
2. Put the salmon on the prepared baking sheet. Season with ¼ teaspoon of salt and the pepper.
3. Transfer the baking sheet to the oven, and bake for 15 to 20 minutes, or until the salmon flakes with a fork. Remove from the oven.
4. Remove the salmon flesh from the skin. Transfer the flesh to a bowl, removing any bones.
5. Mix in the bread crumbs, egg, garlic, dill, and remaining ¼ teaspoon of salt.
6. Form the mixture into 4 patties.
7. In a large skillet, heat the oil over medium heat.
8. Add the patties, and cook for 5 to 6 minutes, or until browned. Flip, and cook on the other side for 3 to 5 minutes. Remove from the heat.

Nutrition Info:
- Per Serving: Calories: 294 ; Fat: 16 g ;Cholesterol:0mg ;Sodium: 458 mg

Walnut-Crusted Halibut

Servings: 2
Cooking Time: 15 Min
Ingredients:
- Aluminum foil
- 1 tbsp whole-grain mustard
- 1 tsp organic honey
- 1 tsp olive oil
- 1 tbsp garlic, minced
- ½ tsp ground black pepper
- 2 (4 oz) halibut fillets, skin on, scaled
- 2 tbsp unsalted walnuts, roughly chopped

Directions:
1. Heat the oven to 425°F, gas mark 7. Line a baking sheet with aluminum foil.
2. In a medium-sized mixing bowl, add together the whole-grain mustard, organic honey, olive oil, minced garlic, and ground black pepper. Mix to combine. Coat the fish fillets evenly with the mustard mixture, and place them on the baking sheet.
3. Sprinkle each fillet with 1 tbsp of chopped walnuts, and cook for 12 to 15 minutes, until the walnuts are browned, and the fish is easily flaked with a fork. Serve warm.

Nutrition Info:
- Per Serving: Calories: 208 ; Fat: 10 g ;Cholesterol: 82 mg ;Sodium: 215 mg

Salmon En Papillote With Sugar Snap Peas, Tomatoes, And Thyme

Servings: 2
Cooking Time: 15 Minutes
Ingredients:
- 2 (4-ounce) salmon fillets, scaled
- ¼ teaspoon freshly ground black pepper
- 8 chopped thyme sprigs, divided
- 3 tablespoons lemon juice
- ½ cup sugar snap peas
- ½ cup cherry tomatoes, halved

Directions:
1. Preheat the oven to 400°F. Line a baking sheet with parchment paper.
2. Create two envelopes from parchment paper. To make one, take a medium-size piece of parchment paper (about 6 inches), fold it in half and make a sharp crease. Cut it into a half-moon shape with the closed section facing you.
3. Place 1 fish fillet in each envelope and top it with 4 chopped thyme sprigs, ⅛ teaspoon of pepper, and 1½ tablespoons of lemon juice. Divide the sugar snap peas and cherry tomatoes between the envelopes.
4. Close the envelopes tightly by pinching together the edges of the parchment paper.
5. Cook for 10 to 15 minutes, then carefully open the envelopes and ensure the fish is flaky. Serve with the side dish of your choice.

Nutrition Info:
- Per Serving: Calories: 152 ; Fat: 5 g ;Cholesterol: 55 mg;Sodium: 178 mg

Rosemary-Lemon Salmon

Servings: 4
Cooking Time: 25 Min
Ingredients:
- 1 pound sustainably sourced fresh, skin-on salmon fillets
- Zest and juice of ½ lemon (about 1½ tablespoons juice)
- 1 garlic clove, minced
- ¼ teaspoon kosher salt
- Freshly ground black pepper
- 2 fresh rosemary sprigs or 1 teaspoon dried rosemary
- 1 tablespoon extra-virgin olive oil (optional)

Directions:
1. Set the oven rack to the second-highest level, and preheat the broiler.
2. Line a rimmed baking sheet with aluminum foil. Place the salmon, skin-side down, on the sheet. Top with the lemon zest and juice, garlic, salt, and pepper. Lay the rosemary sprigs on top. Drizzle with olive oil (if using).
3. Broil the salmon for 5 minutes, then move to a lower rack and reduce the heat to 325°F.
4. Cook for another 8 to 10 minutes, until the salmon is nearly done (see the Cooking Tip). Let the fish rest, tented with foil, for 5 minutes before serving.

Nutrition Info:
- Per Serving: Calories: 193 ; Fat: 11 g ;Cholesterol: 62 mg ;Sodium: 171 mg

Salmon Sage Bake

Servings: 2
Cooking Time: 15 Min
Ingredients:
- Aluminum foil
- 10 broccoli florets
- ¼ tsp ground black pepper
- 1 lime, divided
- 2 (4 oz) salmon fillets, skin removed
- 2 tbsp whole-grain mustard
- ¼ cup sage, finely chopped

Directions:
1. Heat the oven to 375°F, gas mark 5. Line a baking sheet with aluminum foil.
2. Place broccoli florets on the baking sheet, and season with ground black pepper. Divide the broccoli into two beds; five florets for each fish.
3. Cut the lime in half, and cut one half into slices. Reserve the other half of the lime for after cooking.
4. Place the lime slices on top of the broccoli florets, and then place the salmon fillets on top of the limes.
5. In a small mixing bowl, add together the whole-grain mustard and chopped sage. Mix to combine. Evenly spread the mustard mixture on top of each salmon fillet.
6. Cook for 15 minutes, until the fish becomes opaque, and flakes easily with a fork.
7. Squeeze the lime juice from the reserved lime half onto both fillets, and serve warm.

Nutrition Info:
- Per Serving: Calories: 171 ; Fat: 5 g ;Cholesterol: 55 mg ;Sodium: 76 mg

"Home Late" Pantry Tilapia With Veggie Pasta

Servings: 4
Cooking Time: 20 Min

Ingredients:
- 8 ounces uncooked egg noodles
- 5 cups frozen vegetables of your choice
- 1 tablespoon canola or sunflower oil
- 1 pound sustainably sourced tilapia fillets, fresh or frozen and thawed
- ¼ teaspoon kosher salt
- Freshly ground black pepper
- 1 tablespoon extra-virgin olive oil
- 1 teaspoon dried thyme, oregano, or basil or 1 tablespoon minced fresh herbs
- 10 kalamata olives, pitted and sliced (optional)
- Zest and juice of 1 lemon (about 3 tablespoons lemon juice)

Directions:
1. Preheat the oven to 450°F.
2. Fill a large a pot with water, and bring it to a boil over high heat. Cook the egg noodles to al dente, following the package directions. Add the frozen vegetables during the final 2 to 3 minutes of cooking.
3. While the pasta is cooking, lightly brush a rimmed baking sheet with canola oil. Lay the fish on it, and brush with the rest of the oil. Sprinkle with salt and pepper, and set aside.
4. When you're about to drain the pasta, put the fish in the oven. Bake until it just begins to flake at the edges, 4 to 5 minutes, depending on thickness. The center will still be a bit translucent, but the fish will continue to cook after you take it out of the oven.
5. Meanwhile, transfer the drained pasta and veggies to a large bowl, and toss with the olive oil, herbs, and olives (if using). Add the lemon zest and juice.
6. Use a fork to flake the cooked fish into the pasta.

Nutrition Info:
- Per Serving: Calories: 462 ; Fat: 15 g ;Cholesterol: 100 mg ;Sodium: 419 mg

Open-Faced Lemon Pepper Tuna Melt

Servings: 2
Cooking Time: 15 Min

Ingredients:
- 2 teaspoons Better Butter or nonhydrogenated margarine
- 2 slices sprouted-grain bread
- 1 (5-ounce) can sustainably sourced tuna, packed in water
- 2 teaspoons extra-virgin olive oil
- 2 teaspoons mayonnaise
- 1 teaspoon lemon zest
- 1 tablespoon freshly squeezed lemon juice
- 2 tablespoons finely chopped red onion (optional)
- ½ teaspoon red pepper flakes (optional)
- Freshly ground black pepper
- ¼ cup shredded Cheddar cheese

Directions:
1. Set the oven rack about 6 inches from the heat, and preheat the broiler.
2. Spread butter thinly on both sides of bread. Place the bread on a rimmed baking sheet. Toast the bread under the broiler until it is golden brown on both sides, about 2 minutes on each side. Watch it carefully to make sure it doesn't burn.
3. Drain the tuna well, and mash in a medium bowl with the oil, mayonnaise, lemon zest and juice, red onion and red pepper flakes (if using), and black pepper. Mix well.
4. Divide the tuna mixture between the two slices of bread, making sure the bread is completely covered. Sprinkle with the cheese.
5. Broil until the cheese is melted, 2 to 3 minutes.

Nutrition Info:
- Per Serving: Calories: 336 ; Fat: 19 g ;Cholesterol: 46 mg ;Sodium: 450 mg

Fish And Chips With Homemade Tartar Sauce

Servings: 2
Cooking Time: 15 Minutes
Ingredients:
- 1 large zucchini
- 2 egg whites
- ½ cup almond meal
- 1 large garlic clove, minced
- 1¼ teaspoon dried thyme, divided
- 1¼ teaspoon dried basil, divided
- 2 (4-ounce) cod fillets, skinned and cut into 1-inch strips
- 1 teaspoon avocado oil
- ¼ teaspoon freshly ground black pepper
- 4 tablespoons Tartar Sauce

Directions:
1. Preheat the oven to 425°F. Line a baking sheet with parchment paper.
2. Thinly cut the zucchini into small coins. Press the coins with paper towels to draw out excess moisture. The drier you get the coins, the crispier they'll get.
3. In a medium bowl, beat the egg whites. On a medium shallow plate, combine the almond meal, garlic, 1 teaspoon of thyme, and 1 teaspoon of basil, and mix well.
4. Coat the fish strips on both sides with the egg whites. Dredge the fish strips in the almond meal mixture and coat well.
5. Place each strip separately on the prepared baking sheet.
6. In a medium mixing bowl, combine the oil, pepper, and the remaining ¼ teaspoon of thyme and ¼ teaspoon of basil. Add the zucchini coins and toss to coat evenly. Place separately on the baking sheet.
7. Bake for 12 minutes, flipping the fish halfway through, until lightly golden on each side. The zucchini chips should have no excess oil and be crisp. The zucchini chips can be stored in a zip-top bag or an airtight container for 7 days.

Nutrition Info:
- Per Serving: Calories: 328 ; Fat: 17 g ;Cholesterol: 57 mg;Sodium: 239 mg

Chapter 5 Vegetarian And Vegan Mains Recipes

Lentil, Raisin, And Pecan Stuffed Acorn Squash

Servings: 2
Cooking Time: 40 Minutes
Ingredients:
- 1 large acorn squash
- 2¼ teaspoons ground cinnamon, divided
- 1 cup low-sodium canned, cooked lentils, drained and rinsed
- ¼ cup pecan pieces
- ¼ cup raisins

Directions:
1. Preheat the oven to 400°F. Line a baking sheet with parchment paper.
2. Cut the acorn squash in half and scoop out the seeds. Sprinkle ⅛ teaspoon of cinnamon on the inside of each squash and place them flesh-side down on the baking sheet. Cook for 30 minutes until fork-tender and lightly golden brown.
3. In a medium mixing bowl, mix the lentils, pecans, raisins, and the remaining 2 teaspoons of cinnamon. Scoop evenly into the inside of each squash and bake for an additional 5 to 10 minutes, until the pecans and the top of the lentil mixture are lightly golden. Once ready, place half an acorn squash on each plate and serve. This can also be stored in an airtight container in the refrigerator for up to 3 days.

Nutrition Info:
- Per Serving: Calories: 412 ; Fat: 11 g ;Cholesterol: 0 mg ;Sodium: 18 mg

Garbanzo Bean Curry

Servings: 4
Cooking Time: 30 Min
Ingredients:
- 1 tbsp olive oil
- 1 small onion, finely chopped
- 2 cups stir-fry vegetables, fresh or frozen
- 1 tbsp ginger, grated
- 2 tsp mild curry paste
- 1 tsp ground turmeric
- 1 (14 oz) can diced no-salt-added tomatoes, with their juices
- 1 (15 oz) can garbanzo beans, rinsed and drained
- ¼ cup almond butter
- 2 cups reduced-sodium vegetable stock

Directions:
1. In a large, heavy bottom pan, heat the olive oil over medium-high heat.
2. Add the chopped onion, and cook for 4 to 5 minutes, until translucent.
3. Add the stir-fry vegetables, and cook for 3 to 4 minutes. Add the grated ginger, mild curry paste, and ground turmeric, and cook for 1 minute, mix to combine.
4. Stir in the diced tomatoes with their juice, garbanzo beans, almond butter, and vegetable stock, and allow to boil.
5. Allow to simmer on low, stirring occasionally, for 5 to 10 minutes, until warmed through. Serve hot.

Nutrition Info:
- Per Serving: Calories: 308 ; Fat: 14 g ;Cholesterol: 0 mg ;Sodium: 348 mg

Vegan Jambalaya

Servings: 6
Cooking Time: 6 To 8 Hours
Ingredients:
- 5 cups Savory Vegetable Broth (here) or low-sodium vegetable broth
- 1 (15-ounce) can red kidney beans, drained and rinsed
- 2 cups diced fresh tomatoes with their juices, or 1 (14.5-ounce) can no-salt-added diced tomatoes
- 2 cups long-grain brown rice
- 1 cup ½-inch round okra slices
- 1 cup chopped cashews
- 2 celery stalks, diced
- 1 green bell pepper, diced
- 1 medium onion, diced
- 4 garlic cloves, minced

- 2 tablespoons cayenne hot sauce (or to taste)
- 1 tablespoon extra-virgin olive oil
- 1 tablespoon smoked paprika
- 1 tablespoon ground cumin
- 1 teaspoon dried thyme
- 1 teaspoon dried oregano

Directions:
1. Combine all the ingredients in a 6-quart slow cooker. Cover and cook on low for 6 to 8 hours, until the vegetables and rice are tender and the sauce has thickened. If the rice becomes too dry during cooking, add more broth or water.
2. Serve hot.

Nutrition Info:
- Per Serving: Calories: 504 ; Fat: 16 g ;Cholesterol: 0 mg ;Sodium: 153 mg

Veggie Pizza With Cannellini Bean Crust

Servings: 3
Cooking Time: 15 Minutes
Ingredients:
- 1½ cups no-salt-added canned cannellini beans, drained and rinsed
- ½ cup whole wheat flour
- 2 whole eggs
- 1 tablespoon nutritional yeast
- 4 tablespoons low-sodium tomato sauce
- ½ cup mushrooms, thinly sliced
- ½ cup part-skim mozzarella cheese, shredded
- 2 garlic cloves, minced
- 1 teaspoon garlic powder

Directions:
1. Preheat the oven to 450°F. Line a baking sheet with parchment paper.
2. In a blender, combine the beans, flour, eggs, and nutritional yeast. Blend for about 1 minute until well combined and forms a pasty, doughy consistency.
3. Place the mixture on the prepared baking sheet and spread evenly, about 1-inch thick. The mixture will not be like typical pizza dough; it will be slightly sticky. Use a spatula to spread evenly.
4. Bake for 10 minutes, until the edges are lightly browned and start to lift off the parchment paper.
5. Remove the crust from the oven and add the tomato sauce, mushrooms, cheese, garlic, and garlic powder evenly over the pizza. Bake for an additional 5 minutes, until the cheese has melted. Cut into 8 slices and dig in.

Nutrition Info:
- Per Serving: Calories: 290 ; Fat: 9 g ;Cholesterol: 21 mg ;Sodium: 206 mg

Vegetarian Gyros

Servings: 4
Cooking Time: 10 Min
Ingredients:
- 2 tbsp olive oil
- 16 oz whole white mushrooms, sliced
- 2 large green bell peppers, seedless and sliced
- 1 tbsp low-sodium dark soy sauce
- ½ tsp cayenne pepper
- 4 whole-wheat pita rounds
- ½ cup hummus

Directions:
1. Heat the olive oil in a large heavy bottom pan over high heat.
2. Add the sliced mushrooms and sliced green bell peppers, fry for 5 to 7 minutes, or until tender.
3. Turn the heat off and add the dark soy sauce and cayenne pepper. Mix continuously until the soy sauce simmers away.
4. Divide the mushroom mixture among the whole-wheat pitas and spread 1 tbsp of hummus on top. Serve cold.

Nutrition Info:
- Per Serving: Calories: 179 ; Fat: 10 g ;Cholesterol: 0mg ;Sodium: 350 mg

Vegan Chickpea Chili

Servings: 4
Cooking Time: 37 Minutes
Ingredients:
- 4 cups Zesty Carrot Tomato Sauce
- 1 (14.5-ounce) can low-sodium chickpeas, drained and rinsed
- ½ cup dried red lentils
- 1 tablespoon ground cumin
- 4 loose cups baby spinach
- Red pepper flakes (optional)

Directions:
1. Pour the tomato sauce into the Instant Pot and add the chickpeas, lentils, cumin, and baby spinach. Stir to combine.
2. Lock the lid into place. Select Pressure Cook and cook on high pressure for 1 minute. When the cooking is complete, quick release the pressure and remove the lid.
3. Garnish with red pepper flakes, if desired, and serve.

Nutrition Info:
- Per Serving: Calories: 303 ; Fat: 5 g ;Cholesterol: 0mg ;Sodium: 405 mg

Cauliflower, Tomato, And Green Pea Curry

Servings: 4
Cooking Time: 25 Minutes
Ingredients:
- 1 shallot, chopped (about ¼ cup)
- 2 garlic cloves, minced
- 1 teaspoon grated ginger
- 1¼ cups unsweetened oat milk
- 1 tablespoon plus ½ teaspoon curry powder
- ½ teaspoon freshly ground black pepper
- 1 (15-ounce) can no-salt-added diced tomatoes
- 2 cups frozen green peas
- 1 head cauliflower, cut into 2-inch florets

Directions:
1. In a large pot over medium heat, cook the shallot, garlic, and ginger for about 3 minutes until translucent and fragrant.
2. Add the oat milk, curry powder, and pepper to the pot and mix. Then add the tomatoes, green peas, and cauliflower. Combine and coat the ingredients well.
3. Bring the pot to a boil, then cover and simmer on medium-low heat for 20 minutes, until the dish is fragrant and the cauliflower is tender. Serve the mixture over ½ cup of a whole grain or as is. This dish can also be stored in the refrigerator for up to 5 days, or in the freezer for up to 3 months.

Nutrition Info:
- Per Serving: Calories: 159 ; Fat: 3 g ;Cholesterol: 0 mg ;Sodium: 188 mg

Pantry Beans And Rice

Servings: 3
Cooking Time: 25 Min
Ingredients:
- ¾ cup uncooked parboiled brown rice
- 2 teaspoons extra-virgin olive oil
- 1 cup fresh or frozen chopped onion
- 1 (15-ounce) can no-salt-added pinto beans, rinsed and drained
- 1 (14-ounce) can no-salt-added diced tomatoes
- ⅔ cup spicy salsa
- 1 cup frozen broccoli florets
- 1 tablespoon freshly squeezed lime juice
- ⅔ cup shredded aged Cheddar cheese
- ½ teaspoon red pepper flakes (optional)

Directions:
1. Cook the rice according to the package directions.
2. In a large skillet, heat the oil over medium-high heat. Add the onion and cook until soft, 4 to 5 minutes. Then add the beans, tomatoes with their juice, and salsa. Bring to a boil.
3. Add the broccoli, and when the liquid returns to a boil, turn the heat to low and simmer for 2 to 3 minutes. Remove from the heat when the broccoli is crisp-tender but still bright green.
4. Add the rice when it's done cooking. Stir in the lime juice, and top with the shredded Cheddar and red pepper flakes (if using).

Nutrition Info:
- Per Serving: Calories: 479 ; Fat: 14 g ;Cholesterol: 25 mg ;Sodium: 442 mg

Vegan Red Beans And Rice

Servings: 8
Cooking Time: 7 To 8 Hours
Ingredients:
- 1 pound dried kidney beans, soaked overnight and drained
- 6 cups Savory Vegetable Broth (here) or low-sodium vegetable broth
- 1 (14.5-ounce) can no-salt-added fire-roasted tomatoes
- 1 onion, diced
- 1 bell pepper (any color), diced
- 4 garlic cloves, minced
- 1 teaspoon Creole seasoning (or to taste)
- 2 bay leaves
- 1 teaspoon dried thyme
- 1 teaspoon dried oregano
- ½ teaspoon smoked paprika
- 2 cups brown rice, cooked according to package directions

Directions:
1. Put the beans, broth, tomatoes, onion, bell pepper, garlic, Creole seasoning, bay leaves, thyme, oregano, and paprika in a 6-quart slow cooker and stir to combine. Cover and cook on low for 7 to 8 hours.
2. Remove and discard the bay leaves. Serve hot over the brown rice.

Nutrition Info:
- Per Serving: Calories: 380 ; Fat: 1 g ;Cholesterol: 0 mg ;Sodium: 196 mg

Tahini And Black Bean–Stuffed Sweet Potatoes

Servings: 4
Cooking Time: 30 Minutes
Ingredients:
- 4 medium sweet potatoes
- 1 tablespoon extra-virgin olive oil, divided
- 2 cups broccoli florets
- Salt
- Freshly ground black pepper
- 1 (15-ounce) can low-sodium black beans, drained and rinsed
- ½ cup Tahini Dressing
- 2 scallions, green and white parts, sliced

Directions:
1. Preheat the oven to 375°F.
2. Using a fork, prick the sweet potatoes 2 or 3 times.
3. Rub the skin with ½ tablespoon of oil.
4. Put the sweet potatoes on a baking sheet.
5. Transfer the baking sheet to the oven, and bake for 20 to 30 minutes, depending on their size, or until the sweet potatoes are easily pierced using a fork.
6. Meanwhile, in a medium bowl, toss together the broccoli and remaining ½ tablespoon of oil. Season lightly with salt and pepper.
7. After the sweet potatoes have been cooking for about 10 minutes, add the broccoli to the baking sheet alongside the sweet potatoes, and roast for 20 minutes, or until the broccoli is tender and browned. Remove the baking sheet from the oven.
8. Slice the sweet potatoes lengthwise to open them up.
9. Top with the beans, then the broccoli.
10. Drizzle with the tahini dressing. Season with pepper.
11. Serve the sweet potatoes warm, garnished with the scallions.

Nutrition Info:
- Per Serving: Calories: 368 ; Fat: 15 g ;Cholesterol: 0mg ;Sodium: 564 mg

Sweet Spot Lentil Salad

Servings: 3
Cooking Time: 20 Min
Ingredients:
- For the dressing
- 3 tablespoons apple cider vinegar
- 2 tablespoons extra-virgin olive oil
- 1 teaspoon water
- 1 teaspoon Dijon mustard
- ¼ teaspoon salt
- ¼ teaspoon freshly ground black pepper
- For the salad
- 1 (15-ounce) can lentils, rinsed and drained
- 1 red bell pepper, seeded and chopped
- ½ cup frozen corn kernels, thawed
- ½ cup chopped snap peas
- ½ cup diced Jarlsberg cheese
- ¼ cup chopped fresh cilantro

Directions:
1. In a large bowl, whisk together the vinegar, oil, water, mustard, salt, and pepper.
2. Add the lentils, bell pepper, corn, snap peas, cheese, and cilantro, and toss with the dressing.

Nutrition Info:
- Per Serving: Calories: 440 ; Fat: 17 g ;Cholesterol: 20mg ;Sodium: 422 mg

Cannellini Bean Pizza

Servings: 3
Cooking Time: 15 Min
Ingredients:
- Aluminum foil
- 1½ cups canned cannellini beans, drained and rinsed
- ½ cup whole-wheat flour
- 2 large whole eggs
- 1 tbsp nutritional yeast
- 4 tbsp low-sodium tomato puree
- ½ cup whole white mushrooms, thinly sliced
- ½ cup reduced fat cheese blend, shredded
- 1 tbsp garlic, minced
- 1 tsp garlic powder

Directions:
1. Warm the oven to 450°F, gas mark 8. Line a baking sheet with aluminum foil.
2. In a food processor or blender, combine the cannellini beans, whole-wheat flour, whole eggs, and nutritional yeast. Process for 1 minute until it forms a doughy consistency.
3. Place the bean mixture on the baking sheet, and spread evenly. The mixture will not be like pizza dough; it will be slightly sticky. Use a spatula to spread evenly.
4. Bake for 10 minutes, until the edges are lightly browned.
5. Remove the base from the oven, and spread the tomato puree, sliced mushrooms, cheese blend, minced garlic, and garlic powder evenly over the pizza.
6. Bake for 5 minutes, until the cheese has melted. Cut into 8 slices, and serve warm.

Nutrition Info:
- Per Serving: Calories: 290 ; Fat: 9 g ;Cholesterol: 21 mg ;Sodium: 206 mg

Chickpea And Lentil Ratatouille

Servings: 4
Cooking Time: 51 Minutes
Ingredients:
- 5 cups Ratatouille Base
- 1 (14.5-ounce) can low-sodium chickpeas, drained and rinsed
- ½ cup dried red lentils
- 1 tablespoon ground cumin
- 2 cups baby spinach

Directions:
1. Pour the ratatouille base into the Instant Pot. Add the chickpeas, lentils, cumin, and spinach and stir to combine.
2. Lock the lid into place. Select Pressure Cook and cook on high pressure for 1 minute. When the cooking is complete, quick release the pressure, remove the lid, and serve.

Nutrition Info:
- Per Serving: Calories: 323 ; Fat: 6 g ;Cholesterol: 0 mg ;Sodium: 292 mg

Chickpea And Spinach Saag

Servings: 4
Cooking Time: 8 Minutes
Ingredients:

- 2 teaspoons avocado oil
- 3 garlic cloves, crushed and diced
- 1 (16-ounce) bag frozen spinach
- 1 teaspoon curry powder
- ½ cup unsweetened oat milk
- 2 cups canned chickpeas, drained and rinsed
- ¼ teaspoon freshly ground black pepper

Directions:

1. In a medium pot, heat the oil over medium heat and add the garlic. Cook for about 1 minute, until the garlic sizzles.
2. Add the spinach and curry powder and cook for 2 minutes, until the spinach defrosts.
3. Add the oat milk, chickpeas, and pepper. Cover and cook for about 5 minutes until the liquid bubbles, the chickpeas soften, and the dish becomes fragrant. Serve warm or store in an airtight container in the refrigerator for up to 4 days.

Nutrition Info:

- Per Serving: Calories: 185 ; Fat: 6 g ;Cholesterol: 0 mg ;Sodium: 104 mg

White Bean Soup With Orange And Celery

Servings: 6
Cooking Time: 25 Minutes
Ingredients:

- 2 tablespoons extra-virgin olive oil, plus more for serving
- 1 large onion, chopped
- 1½ cups chopped celery
- ½ teaspoon salt
- ½ teaspoon freshly ground black pepper
- 4 cups water
- 2 (15-ounce) cans white beans, drained and rinsed
- 1 teaspoon dried oregano
- Zest of ½ medium orange
- Juice of 1 medium orange

Directions:

1. In a large saucepan, heat the oil over medium-high heat.
2. Add the onion and celery. Cook for 4 to 6 minutes, or until lightly browned and softened. Season with the salt and pepper.
3. Add the water, beans, and oregano. Bring to a boil.
4. Reduce the heat to a simmer. Cook for 15 minutes, or until the flavors meld. Remove from the heat.
5. Add the orange zest and orange juice.
6. Serve the soup topped with more oil if desired.

Nutrition Info:

- Per Serving: Calories: 188 ; Fat: 5 g ;Cholesterol: 0mg ;Sodium: 217 mg

One-Skillet Southwest Quinoa And Vegetables

Cooking Time: 30 Minutes
Ingredients:

- ½ tablespoon olive oil
- ½ cup chopped sweet onion
- ¼ cup chopped red bell pepper
- 1 cup chopped tomato, with juices
- ½ cup quinoa, rinsed
- ½ cup water
- ½ cup corn kernels, fresh or thawed from frozen
- 1 (15-ounce) can black beans, drained and rinsed
- ½ teaspoon chili powder
- ½ teaspoon ground cumin
- Salt
- Freshly ground black pepper
- ¼ cup chopped fresh cilantro, for garnish (optional)
- Avocado slices, for garnish (optional)
- 1 lime, sliced, for garnish (optional)

Directions:

1. In a large skillet, heat the olive oil over medium heat. Sauté the onion and bell pepper for 3 to 4 minutes, or until softened.
2. Add the tomato with its juices, quinoa, water, corn, black beans, chili powder, and cumin and season with salt

and pepper. Bring the quinoa mixture to a boil. Decrease the heat and simmer, covered, for 20 to 25 minutes, or until the liquid has been absorbed.

3. Remove from the heat and divide between two serving plates. Garnish with the cilantro, avocado slices, and fresh lime (if using) and serve warm.

Nutrition Info:
- Per Serving: Calories: 533 ; Fat: 8 g ;Cholesterol: 0 mg ;Sodium: 102 mg

Spicy Bean And Rice–Stuffed Peppers

Servings: 6
Cooking Time: 7 To 8 Hours
Ingredients:
- 1 (15-ounce) can no-salt-added black beans, drained and rinsed
- 1 (15-ounce) can no-salt-added pinto beans, drained and rinsed
- 1 (4-ounce) can diced green chiles
- 1¼ cups Spicy Salsa (here) or store-bought salsa
- 1 cup frozen corn
- 1 cup quick-cooking (Minute) brown rice
- 1 cup 2% shredded Cheddar cheese, divided
- 2 teaspoons ground cumin
- 2 teaspoons chili powder
- 6 bell peppers (any color), tops cut off, seeded, membrane removed
- 1 cup water

Directions:
1. In a large bowl, mix together the black beans, pinto beans, chiles, salsa, corn, rice, ¾ cup of cheese, cumin, and chili powder. Fill each bell pepper with the mixture and stand each pepper in a 6-quart slow cooker top-side up. Pour the water in the space between the peppers, being careful not to pour it over the peppers or filling.
2. Cover and cook on low for 7 to 8 hours.
3. Sprinkle each pepper with the remaining ¼ cup of cheese. Cover the slow cooker and cook an additional 3 to 4 minutes, or until cheese is melted.
4. Serve hot.

Nutrition Info:
- Per Serving: Calories: 294 ; Fat: 5 g ;Cholesterol: 13 mg ;Sodium: 396 mg

Feta And Black Bean–Stuffed Zucchini

Servings: 4
Cooking Time: 25 Minutes
Ingredients:
- 4 medium zucchini, halved lengthwise
- 2 tablespoons extra-virgin olive oil, divided
- 1 (15-ounce) can black beans, drained and rinsed
- 1 large tomato, chopped
- ½ cup crumbled feta cheese
- ¼ cup chopped fresh mint leaves
- Salt
- Freshly ground black pepper

Directions:
1. Preheat the oven to 400°F.
2. Using a spoon, remove the center of each zucchini, leaving about ½ inch of zucchini skin and flesh. Reserve the flesh.
3. Rub the halved zucchini all over with 1 tablespoon of oil.
4. Place the zucchini, cut-side down, on a baking sheet.
5. Transfer the baking sheet to the oven, and bake for 15 minutes, or until the zucchini is just tender. Remove from the oven, leaving the oven on. Flip the zucchini over so the cut side is up.
6. Meanwhile, chop the reserved zucchini flesh.
7. In a skillet, heat the remaining 1 tablespoon of oil over medium heat.
8. Add the chopped zucchini, and cook for 1 to 2 minutes, or until tender.
9. Add the beans and tomato, and cook for 3 to 5 minutes, or until heated through and the tomato has released its juices.
10. Stir in the cheese and mint. Remove from the heat. Season with salt and pepper.
11. Divide the filling among the zucchini.
12. Return the baking sheet to the oven, and bake for 10 minutes, or until the filling has lightly browned. Remove from the oven.

Nutrition Info:
- Per Serving: Calories: 236 ; Fat: 12 g ;Cholesterol: 0mg ;Sodium: 229 mg

Chickpea Sloppy Joes

Servings: 6
Cooking Time: 7 To 8 Hours

Ingredients:
- 4 cups Savory Vegetable Broth (here) or low-sodium vegetable broth
- 2 (15-ounce) cans chickpeas, drained and rinsed
- 1 cup brown lentils, rinsed and picked over
- 1 cup Rustic Marinara Sauce (here)
- 2 medium carrots, diced
- 1 medium onion, diced
- 1 bell pepper (any color), diced
- 4 garlic cloves, minced
- 4 tablespoons tomato paste
- 1 tablespoon molasses
- 1 tablespoon apple cider vinegar
- ½ tablespoon dried mustard (or more to taste)
- Freshly ground black pepper

Directions:
1. Combine all the ingredients to a 6-quart slow cooker. Cover and cook on low for 7 to 8 hours until the lentils are tender and the sauce has thickened.
2. In the last 30 minutes of cooking, open the slow cooker and mash one-quarter to one-third of the filling with a potato masher. Stir, cover, and cook for the remaining 30 minutes.
3. Serve hot on toasted whole-wheat buns with your favorite toppings or in lettuce leaves, if desired.

Nutrition Info:
- Per Serving: Calories: 262 ; Fat:0 g ;Cholesterol: 0 mg ;Sodium: 215 mg

Mushroom, Zucchini, And Chickpea Stuffed Tomatoes

Servings: 4
Cooking Time: 20 Minutes

Ingredients:
- 4 large, firm beefsteak tomatoes
- Nonstick avocado oil cooking spray
- 2 teaspoons avocado oil
- 2 garlic cloves, minced
- 1½ cups diced zucchini
- 2 cups diced mushrooms
- ½ teaspoon freshly ground black pepper
- 2 cups low-sodium chickpeas, drained and rinsed

Directions:
1. Set an oven rack 6 inches below the broiler. Preheat the oven to 400°F.
2. Cut ½ to 1 inch off the top of the tomatoes, removing the stems. With a spoon, gently scoop out the pulp, stopping about 1 inch from the bottoms. Save the tomato pulp. If the tomato is too firm, you can use a knife to score the pulp and it should easily come out. Spray an oven-safe dish with cooking spray (or evenly grease with 1 teaspoon of avocado oil). Place the tomatoes in the dish and surround them with the tomato pulp.
3. In a medium skillet, heat the oil over medium heat and add the garlic. Sauté for about 1 minute until the garlic is sizzling. Add the zucchini, mushrooms, and pepper and cook on medium heat for 2 to 3 minutes until lightly browned and caramelized. Turn off the heat and mix the chickpeas into the skillet.
4. Fill each tomato with the mixture (about ¾ cup each). If there is extra mixture, place it in the dish with the pulp surrounding the tomatoes.
5. Cook in the oven for 10 minutes, then switch to broil and cook for 5 minutes more until the mixture is lightly browned and the tomato has slightly browned edges. Serve warm or store in an airtight container in the refrigerator for up to 4 days.

Nutrition Info:
- Per Serving: Calories: 187 ; Fat: 5 g ;Cholesterol: 0 mg ;Sodium: 21 mg

White Bean Cabbage Casserole

Servings: 6
Cooking Time: 7 To 8 Hours

Ingredients:

- 2 (15-ounce) cans cannellini beans, drained and rinsed, or 1½ to 2 cups Savory Great Northern Beans (here)
- 1 small head of cabbage, cored and leaves sliced (about 5 to 6 cups total)
- 1 (14.5-ounce) can no-salt-added diced tomatoes
- 2 cups riced cauliflower
- 1 cup Savory Vegetable Broth (here) or low-sodium vegetable broth
- 1 onion, diced
- 4 garlic cloves, finely chopped
- 2 tablespoons extra-virgin olive oil
- 1 tablespoon Italian seasoning
- 1 teaspoon smoked paprika
- Freshly ground black pepper

Directions:

1. Combine all the ingredients to a 6-quart slow cooker. Cover and cook on low for 7 to 8 hours.
2. Serve hot.

Nutrition Info:

- Per Serving: Calories: 202 ; Fat: 5 g ;Cholesterol: 0 mg ;Sodium: 51 mg

Pile-It-High Veggie Sandwich

Servings: 2
Cooking Time: 15 Min

Ingredients:

- 2 teaspoons red wine vinegar
- 1 teaspoon extra-virgin olive oil
- ¼ teaspoon ground cumin
- ⅓ cup shredded carrot (about 1 carrot)
- 2 tablespoons hummus, divided
- 4 slices whole-grain multigrain bread
- ½ avocado, sliced
- 6 (½-inch-thick) slices Simple Roasted Peppers or jarred roasted red peppers, drained well
- 4 green lettuce leaves

Directions:

1. In a small bowl, whisk together the vinegar, oil, and cumin. Add the carrot and toss well, then set aside to marinate for 10 minutes.
2. Spread 1 tablespoon of hummus on each of two slices of bread.
3. Divide the avocado slices between the other two pieces of bread. Top with the roasted peppers and lettuce.
4. Drain the carrots, and add them on top of the lettuce. Close the sandwiches and enjoy.

Nutrition Info:

- Per Serving: Calories: 384 ; Fat: 16 g ;Cholesterol: 0 mg ;Sodium: 463 mg

Mujaddara

Servings: 6
Cooking Time: 40 Minutes

Ingredients:

- 5 cups water
- 1 teaspoon salt, divided
- 1 cup brown basmati rice
- 1 cup dried brown lentils
- ¼ cup extra-virgin olive oil
- 2 large onions, thinly sliced
- ½ cup chopped fresh parsley
- 6 scallions, green and white parts, sliced, divided
- Freshly ground black pepper

Directions:

1. In a large saucepan, bring the water and ¾ teaspoon of salt to a boil over high heat.
2. Add the rice, and cook for 10 minutes, lowering the heat to maintain a simmer.
3. Add the lentils, and return to a simmer. Cover the saucepan, and simmer over medium-low heat for 20 to 25 minutes, or until the lentils and rice are tender. Remove from the heat. Drain any remaining liquid. Let rest for 10 minutes.
4. Meanwhile, in a large skillet, heat the oil over medium-high heat. Line a plate with paper towels.
5. Once the oil is hot, add the onions, and cook, stirring regularly, for 20 to 25 minutes, or until well browned. Remove from the heat. Using a slotted spoon, transfer the

onions to the prepared plate. Sprinkle with the remaining ¼ teaspoon of salt.
6. Gently mix half of the onions, the parsley, and half of the scallions into the lentils and rice, reserving the remaining onions and scallions for garnish.
7. Serve the lentils and rice topped with the reserved onions and scallions. Season with pepper.

Nutrition Info:
- Per Serving: Calories: 333 ; Fat: 10 g ;Cholesterol: 0mg ;Sodium: 399 mg

Corn, Spinach, And Mushroom Soup

Servings: 4
Cooking Time: 16 Minutes
Ingredients:
- 2 teaspoons olive oil
- 2 cups frozen corn kernels
- 1 teaspoon ground cumin
- 1 teaspoon garlic powder
- ½ teaspoon chili powder (optional)
- 8 ounces mushrooms, sliced
- 1 tablespoon white wine vinegar or rice vinegar
- 4 cups low-sodium chicken broth
- 1½ cups low-sodium black beans, drained and rinsed
- ⅛ teaspoon salt
- 4 cups baby spinach

Directions:
1. Select Sauté and wait 30 seconds for the Instant Pot to warm. Pour in the oil and heat for 30 seconds, until it sizzles. Stir in the corn, cumin, garlic powder, and chili powder (if using). Sauté for 3 minutes, until fragrant, then add the mushrooms and vinegar and cook for 3 minutes more, until the mushrooms start to cook down.
2. Add the broth, beans, and salt and cook for 3 minutes more, until the mixture comes to a boil. Add the spinach, 1 cup at a time, and cook for 1 minute, until it is wilted.
3. Divide evenly among four bowls and serve.

Nutrition Info:
- Per Serving: Calories: 224 ; Fat: 3 g ;Cholesterol: 0 mg ;Sodium: 184 mg

Tofu And Veggie "Ramen" With Soba Noodles

Servings: 4
Cooking Time: 4 Minutes
Ingredients:
- 2 teaspoons olive oil
- 2 large red bell peppers, thinly sliced
- 1 cup coarsely chopped chard
- 1 cup chopped mushrooms
- 1 garlic clove, crushed
- 1 teaspoon grated fresh ginger
- 4 cups water
- 1 tablespoon low-sodium tamari
- ¼ cup frozen corn kernels
- 6 ounces soba noodles
- 1 pound firm tofu, cut into cubes
- 4 scallions (green parts only), chopped, for garnish
- 1 medium avocado, cubed

Directions:
1. Select Sauté and wait 30 seconds for the Instant Pot to warm. Pour in the oil and heat for 30 seconds, until it sizzles. Add the bell peppers, chard, and mushrooms. Sauté for 12 minutes, until the veggies have softened, then add the garlic and ginger and sauté for another minute, until fragrant.
2. Add the water, tamari, corn, and soba noodles. Be sure to lay the noodles flat so they are completely covered with the water.
3. Set the trivet in the center of the pot. Place the tofu in a 6-inch round cake pan and cover with aluminum foil, then place the pan on the trivet.
4. Lock the lid into place. Select Pressure Cook and cook on high pressure for 4 minutes. When the cooking is complete, allow the pressure to release naturally for 10 minutes, then quick release any remaining pressure and remove the lid.
5. Divide the broth, noodles, and tofu evenly among four bowls and garnish with the scallions and avocado.

Nutrition Info:
- Per Serving: Calories: 375 ; Fat: 15 g ;Cholesterol: 0 mg ;Sodium: 569 mg

Butter Bean Penne

Servings: 4
Cooking Time: 15 Min

Ingredients:
- 8 oz whole-wheat penne
- 2 tbsp coconut oil
- 3 cups collard greens, stemmed and chopped
- 1 (15 oz) can low-sodium diced tomatoes, drained
- 1 (15 oz) can low-sodium butter beans, drained and rinsed
- 1 tsp dried thyme
- Fine sea salt
- Ground black pepper

Directions:
1. Fill a large stockpot with water, and bring to a boil.
2. Cook the pasta for 8 minutes, or according to the package instructions, until al dente. Remove from the heat, and reserve ½ cup of the water, then drain the pasta.
3. Heat the coconut oil in a large, heavy bottom pan, over medium heat.
4. Add the chopped collard greens, and fry for 4 to 6 minutes, until wilted.
5. Add the drained diced tomatoes and drained butter beans. Cook for 3 to 5 minutes, or until heated through. Season with dried thyme, fine sea salt, and ground black pepper to taste.
6. Mix in the cooked pasta, and ¼ cup of the reserved water. Cook for 1 minute, stirring frequently, until heated through. Add the remaining ¼ cup reserved water if you prefer a thinner sauce. Remove from the heat, and serve immediately.

Nutrition Info:
- Per Serving: Calories: 435 ; Fat: 9 g ;Cholesterol: 0 mg ;Sodium: 208 mg

Spicy Spinach And Almond Stir-Fry

Cooking Time: 10 Minutes

Ingredients:
- 3 teaspoons olive oil, divided 2 eggs, beaten
- 2 garlic cloves, minced
- ¾ cup chopped scallions
- 1 cup thinly sliced Brussels sprouts
- 4 cups baby spinach
- ¼ cup sliced almonds
- 2 cups cooked and chilled brown rice
- 2 teaspoons reduced-sodium tamari or soy sauce
- 2 teaspoons sriracha
- 1 lime, halved
- ¼ cup chopped fresh cilantro, for garnish

Directions:
1. Heat a large (12-inch or wider) wok or nonstick frying pan over medium-high heat. Once the pan is hot enough that a drop of water sizzles on contact, add 1 teaspoon of olive oil. Pour in the eggs and cook, stirring occasionally, until the eggs are scrambled and lightly set, about 3 minutes. Transfer the eggs to a medium bowl.
2. Add 1 teaspoon of olive oil to the pan and add the garlic, scallions, and Brussels sprouts. Cook, stirring frequently, for 30 seconds, or until fragrant. Add the spinach and continue to cook, stirring frequently, for about 2 minutes, or until the spinach is wilted and tender. Transfer the mixture to the bowl of eggs.
3. Add the almonds to the pan and cook, stirring frequently, for about 1 minute, or until they are crisp and lightly browned. Add the remaining 1 teaspoon of olive oil and the rice to the pan and cook, stirring occasionally, for about 3 minutes until the rice is hot.
4. Pour the contents of the bowl back into the pan. Add the tamari, sriracha, and juice from half a lime. Stir to combine and remove from the heat.
5. Cut the remaining lime half into wedges then divide the stir-fry into individual bowls. Garnish with the lime wedges and a sprinkling of cilantro. Serve immediately.

Nutrition Info:
- Per Serving: Calories: 587 ; Fat: 20 g ;Cholesterol: 164 mg ;Sodium: 557 mg

Chickpea Tikka Masala

Servings: 6
Cooking Time: 7 To 8 Hours
Ingredients:
- 1 (28-ounce) can no-salt-added fire-roasted tomatoes
- 3 (15-ounce) cans chickpeas, drained and rinsed
- 1 cup Savory Vegetable Broth (here), low-sodium vegetable broth, or water
- 1 cup green peas (thawed if frozen)
- 1 onion, diced
- 1 red bell pepper, diced
- 4 garlic cloves, minced
- 2 tablespoons tomato paste
- 2 tablespoons garam masala
- 1 tablespoon minced ginger
- 2 teaspoons extra-virgin olive oil
- Freshly ground black pepper
- 4 cups cauliflower florets
- 1 (13.5-ounce) can light coconut milk

Directions:
1. Put the tomatoes, chickpeas, broth, peas, onion, bell pepper, garlic, tomato paste, garam masala, ginger, olive oil, and black pepper in a 6-quart slow cooker and stir. Cover and cook on low for 7 to 8 hours.
2. Stir in the cauliflower and coconut milk with 30 minutes left of cooking time. Leave the slow cooker uncovered to finish cooking and thicken the sauce.
3. Serve hot over rice, if desired.

Nutrition Info:
- Per Serving: Calories: 304 ; Fat: 5 g ;Cholesterol: 0 mg ;Sodium: 434 mg

Spicy Pear Tacos

Servings: 2
Cooking Time: 10 Min
Ingredients:
- Aluminum foil
- 1 (8 oz) package extra-firm tofu, crumbled
- ¼ cup jalapeño pepper, diced
- 2 tbsp Chile-Lime Glaze, divided
- 2 cups broccoli slaw
- 2 Anjou pears, core removed and diced
- ¼ tsp ground black pepper
- 4 small low-sodium whole wheat taco shells

Directions:
1. Warm the oven to 425°F gas mark 7. Line a baking sheet with aluminum foil.
2. In a medium sized mixing bowl, Add the crumbled tofu, diced jalapeño pepper and 1 tbsp of Chili-Lime glaze to the tofu mixture, mix to combine.
3. Spread the tofu mixture onto the baking sheet and bake for 10 minutes, until lightly browned.
4. In a large sized mixing bowl, add the broccoli slaw, diced pears, ground black pepper, and the remaining 1 tbsp of Chile-Lime glaze and mix well.
5. Divide the tofu mixture among four small whole wheat taco shells and serve warm or cold.

Nutrition Info:
- Per Serving: Calories: 449 ; Fat: 17 g ;Cholesterol: 0mg ;Sodium: 101 mg

Spaghetti Squash Stuffed With Kale, Artichokes, And Chickpeas

Servings: 4
Cooking Time: 50 Minutes
Ingredients:
- 2 small spaghetti squash
- 1 cup water
- 2 tablespoons extra-virgin olive oil
- 2 cups chopped kale
- 1 cup chopped artichoke hearts
- 1 cup canned chickpeas, drained and rinsed
- ¼ teaspoon salt
- ¼ teaspoon freshly ground black pepper
- 1 cup Marinara Sauce

Directions:
1. Preheat the oven to 400°F.
2. Cut the squash in half lengthwise, and using a spoon, remove the seeds.
3. Place the squash pieces, cut-side down, in a large baking dish.

4. Add the water to the dish, and cover with aluminum foil.
5. Transfer the baking dish to the oven, and bake for 35 to 40 minutes, or until the squash is easily pierced with a fork. Remove from the oven, leaving the oven on.
6. Meanwhile, in a skillet, heat the oil over medium heat.
7. Add the kale, and sauté for 2 to 3 minutes, or until wilted.
8. Add the artichoke hearts and chickpeas. Cook for 2 minutes, or until heated through. Remove from the heat.
9. Using a fork, scrape the flesh from the squash to remove it in strands. Save the squash shells.
10. Mix the strands of spaghetti squash with the vegetable and bean mixture. Season with the salt and pepper. Spoon the mixture back into the squash shell.
11. Drizzle each squash piece with ¼ cup of marinara sauce.
12. Return the baking dish to the oven, and bake for 10 minutes, or until everything is heated through. Remove from the oven.

Nutrition Info:
- Per Serving: Calories: 252 ; Fat: 13 g ;Cholesterol: 0mg ;Sodium: 330 mg

Chickpeas, Tomatoes, And Swiss Chard

Servings: 4
Cooking Time: 20 Min
Ingredients:
- 1 bunch Swiss chard
- 2 tablespoons extra-virgin olive oil
- 1 onion, thinly sliced
- 2 garlic cloves, minced
- 1 teaspoon ground cumin
- ½ teaspoon red pepper flakes
- 1 (14-ounce) can diced tomatoes seasoned with basil and garlic
- 1 (15-ounce) can no-salt-added chickpeas, rinsed and drained
- Zest and juice of 1 lemon (about 3 tablespoons juice)
- ½ cup chopped walnuts
- Freshly ground black pepper

Directions:
1. Trim the chard, then chop the stems and leaves; keep the stems and leaves separate.
2. Heat the oil in a large skillet over medium heat. When it is hot, add the onion and garlic and cook, stirring occasionally, for 3 to 4 minutes.
3. Add the chard stems and continue to cook until the onion is softened, 3 to 4 minutes more.
4. Add the cumin and red pepper flakes, and cook for 1 minute. Add the tomatoes with their juice and the chickpeas, and cook until warm, 3 to 4 minutes.
5. Add the chard leaves, cover, and cook until wilted, about 2 minutes.
6. Remove from the heat, and add the lemon zest and juice, walnuts, and pepper.

Nutrition Info:
- Per Serving: Calories: 317 ; Fat: 18 g ;Cholesterol: 0 mg ;Sodium: 482 mg

Broccoli And Pasta With Peanut Sauce

Servings: 4
Cooking Time: 25 Min
Ingredients:
- 8 ounces uncooked whole-wheat rotini
- 1 pint cherry tomatoes
- ⅔ cup reduced-sodium vegetable broth
- ½ cup natural peanut butter
- 3 tablespoons rice vinegar
- 1 tablespoon canola or sunflower oil
- 1 teaspoon toasted sesame oil
- 1½ teaspoons reduced-sodium soy sauce
- 1 garlic clove, chopped
- 3½ cups broccoli florets (about 1 pound)

Directions:
1. Bring a large pot of water to a boil over high heat. Cook the rotini to al dente, according to the package directions.
2. While the pasta is cooking, combine the tomatoes, broth, peanut butter, vinegar, canola oil, sesame oil, soy sauce, and garlic in a medium pot over medium heat. Cook, stirring occasionally, until the tomatoes burst.
3. A few minutes before the pasta is finished cooking, add the broccoli to the pasta pot. When it starts boiling again,

turn it back down and simmer for another 3 minutes. Drain and return the pasta and broccoli to the pasta pot.
4. Add the sauce, and toss to coat.

Nutrition Info:
- Per Serving: Calories: 490 ; Fat: 23 g ;Cholesterol: 0 mg ;Sodium: 210 mg

Pocket Eggs With Sesame Sauce

Cooking Time: 5 Minutes
Ingredients:
- 2 teaspoons low-sodium soy sauce
- 1 teaspoon sesame oil
- 1½ tablespoons rice vinegar
- 1 tablespoon minced scallions
- 2 teaspoons olive oil
- 4 large eggs
- 1 tablespoon black or white sesame seeds
- 1 tablespoon dried basil
- ¼ teaspoon freshly ground black pepper

Directions:
1. In a small bowl, whisk together the soy sauce, sesame oil, vinegar, and scallions. Set it aside.
2. Heat the olive oil in a medium nonstick skillet over medium heat and swirl to coat. Crack 2 eggs into a small bowl then crack the remaining 2 eggs into a second small bowl.
3. Working quickly, pour 2 eggs on one side of the skillet and the other 2 on the opposite side of the skillet. The egg whites will flow together, forming one large piece.
4. Sprinkle the sesame seeds, basil, and pepper over the eggs. Cook until the egg whites are crispy and golden brown on the bottom and the yolks are firmly set, about 3 minutes. Keeping them in one piece, flip the eggs using a wide spatula and cook until the whites turn crispy and golden brown on the other side, 1 to 2 minutes more.
5. Pour the reserved sauce over the eggs. Simmer for 30 seconds, turning the eggs once to coat both sides with sauce. Serve in wedges, drizzled with the pan sauce.

Nutrition Info:
- Per Serving: Calories: 241 ; Fat: 19 g ;Cholesterol: 372 mg ;Sodium: 440 mg

Chickpea Gyros

Servings: 2
Cooking Time: 5 Minutes
Ingredients:
- 1 tablespoon extra-virgin olive oil
- 1 (15-ounce) can low-sodium chickpeas, drained and rinsed
- 1 teaspoon paprika
- ½ teaspoon cayenne pepper
- 2 whole-wheat pita rounds
- ¼ cup Tzatziki

Directions:
1. In a large skillet, heat the oil over medium heat.
2. Add the chickpeas, and sauté for 2 to 3 minutes, or until heated through.
3. Sprinkle with the paprika and cayenne. Mix well. Cook for 30 seconds, or until fragrant. Remove from the heat.
4. Divide the chickpeas between the pitas.
5. Top with the tzatziki.

Nutrition Info:
- Per Serving: Calories:168 ; Fat: 6 g ;Cholesterol: 0mg ;Sodium: 262 mg

Acorn Squash Stuffed With White Beans And Kale

Cooking Time: 25 Minutes
Ingredients:
- 1 medium acorn squash, halved and seeded
- 2½ teaspoons olive oil, divided
- ⅛ teaspoon salt
- ¼ teaspoon freshly ground black pepper, divided
- ¼ cup chopped onion
- 2 garlic cloves, minced
- 1 tablespoon water
- 1 tablespoon tomato paste, no salt added

- 4 cups stemmed and chopped kale
- 1 cup canned white beans, drained and rinsed
- 2 tablespoons wheat germ
- 1 tablespoon dried basil
- 1 teaspoon dried rosemary
- 2 tablespoons feta cheese

Directions:
1. Cut a small slice off the bottom of each squash half so they rest flat. Brush the insides with ½ teaspoon of olive oil, then sprinkle with the salt and ⅛ teaspoon black pepper. Place in an 8-by-8-inch (or similar size) microwave-safe dish. Cover with plastic wrap and microwave on high until the squash is fork-tender, about 12 minutes.
2. Meanwhile, heat 1 teaspoon of olive oil in a large skillet over medium heat. Add the onion and cook, stirring, for 2 to 3 minutes, or until the onion starts to brown. Add the garlic and cook, stirring, for 1 minute. Stir in the water, tomato paste, and the remaining ⅛ teaspoon of pepper. Stir in the kale, cover, and cook for 3 to 5 minutes, or until tender. Stir in the beans and cook until heated through, 1 to 2 minutes more. Remove from the heat.
3. Position a rack in the center of the oven and preheat the broiler.
4. In a bowl, combine the wheat germ, basil, rosemary, feta cheese, and the remaining 1 teaspoon of olive oil. Fill each squash half with half of the kale-bean mixture. Place them in a baking pan or on a baking sheet. Sprinkle them with the wheat germ mixture and broil for 1 to 2 minutes, or until the wheat germ has browned. Serve warm.

Nutrition Info:
- Per Serving: Calories: 401 ; Fat: 10 g ;Cholesterol: 8 mg ;Sodium: 328 mg

Pasta E Fagioli

Servings: 4
Cooking Time: 15 Minutes
Ingredients:
- 8 ounces rotini pasta
- 2 tablespoons extra-virgin olive oil
- 1 bunch kale, stemmed and chopped
- 1 (15-ounce) can low-sodium diced tomatoes, drained
- 1 (15-ounce) can low-sodium white beans, drained and rinsed
- 1 teaspoon dried oregano
- Salt
- Freshly ground black pepper

Directions:
1. Fill a large saucepan with water. Bring to a boil.
2. Cook the pasta according to the package directions, until al dente. Remove from the heat. Reserve about ½ cup of the cooking water, then drain.
3. In a large skillet, heat the oil over medium-high heat.
4. Add the kale, and sauté for 4 to 6 minutes, or until wilted.
5. Add the tomatoes and beans. Cook for 3 to 5 minutes, or until heated through and the tomatoes release some of their water.
6. Season with the oregano, salt, and pepper.
7. Stir the pasta into the skillet along with ¼ cup of the cooking water. Continue cooking, stirring continuously, for 1 more minute, or until heated through. If desired, add the remaining ¼ cup of the cooking water to create a thinner sauce. Remove from the heat.

Nutrition Info:
- Per Serving: Calories: 435 ; Fat: 9 g ;Cholesterol: 0mg ;Sodium: 208 mg

Lentil-Walnut Bolognese

Servings: 4
Cooking Time: 5 Minutes
Ingredients:
- 3 cups Zesty Carrot Tomato Sauce
- 1 cup dried red lentils
- ¼ cup walnuts
- 4 ounces rotini pasta
- 1½ cups water
- 1 tablespoon low-sodium Worcestershire sauce
- 1 teaspoon low-sodium soy sauce

Directions:
1. In the Instant Pot, combine the tomato sauce, lentils, walnuts, pasta, water, Worcestershire sauce, and soy sauce.
2. Lock the lid into place. Select Pressure Cook and cook on high pressure for 5 minutes. When the cooking is complete, allow the pressure to release naturally for 5

minutes, then quick release any remaining pressure and remove the lid.
3. Divide among four bowls and serve warm.

Nutrition Info:
- Per Serving: Calories: 395 ; Fat: 9 g ;Cholesterol: 0 mg ;Sodium: 375 mg

4. Divide among four bowls and garnish with the remaining 2 tablespoons of scallions, black pepper, and red pepper flakes, if desired.

Nutrition Info:
- Per Serving: Calories: 334 ; Fat: 7 g ;Cholesterol: 0 mg ;Sodium: 264 mg

Curried Soup With Cauliflower

Servings: 4
Cooking Time: 4 Minutes
Ingredients:
- 3 teaspoons olive oil, divided
- ½ cup plus 2 tablespoons chopped scallions, divided
- 4 cups low-sodium chicken broth
- 1 pound cauliflower florets
- 1 (15-ounce) can pure pumpkin puree
- 1 tablespoon honey
- ¼ teaspoon salt
- 1½ tablespoons curry powder
- 3 garlic cloves, crushed
- ½ teaspoon ground cinnamon
- ¼ teaspoon ground cumin
- 1 cup dried red lentils
- Freshly ground black pepper
- Red pepper flakes (optional)

Directions:
1. Select Sauté and wait 30 seconds for the Instant Pot to warm. Pour in 2 teaspoons of oil and heat for 30 seconds, until it starts to sizzle. Add ½ cup of scallions and sauté for about 3 minutes, until they start to brown.
2. Add the broth, cauliflower, pumpkin, honey, salt, curry powder, garlic, cinnamon, cumin, and lentils and stir.
3. Lock the lid into place. Select Pressure Cook and cook on high pressure for 4 minutes. When the cooking is complete, allow the pressure to release naturally for 10 minutes, then quick release any remaining pressure and remove the lid. The lentils should mush right into the mixture (the soup should be thick) and the cauliflower should be broken down and soft. Stir in the remaining 1 teaspoon of olive oil.

Lentil And Fennel Salad

Servings: 4
Cooking Time: 20 Minutes
Ingredients:
- 1 cup dried brown or green lentils
- 2 carrots, grated
- 1 fennel bulb, cored and thinly sliced
- ½ cup chopped fresh parsley
- ½ cup Lemon Vinaigrette

Directions:
1. In a large saucepan, cover the lentils with water by a few inches. Bring to a boil over high heat.
2. Reduce the heat to medium. Simmer for 15 to 20 minutes, or until the lentils are tender but not mushy. Remove from the heat. Drain, and rinse with cold water to cool.
3. While the lentils are cooking, in a large bowl, toss together the carrots, fennel, parsley, and vinaigrette. Let sit until the lentils are ready.
4. Add the lentils, and gently mix.

Nutrition Info:
- Per Serving: Calories: 372 ; Fat: 19 g ;Cholesterol: 0mg ;Sodium:284 mg

Vegetable Curry

Servings: 6 To 8
Cooking Time: 7 To 8 Hours

Ingredients:
- 1 (28-ounce) can no-salt-added diced tomatoes
- 1 (15-ounce) can chickpeas, drained and rinsed
- 1 (14-ounce) can light coconut milk
- 4 cups cauliflower florets
- 2 cups Savory Vegetable Broth (here) or low-sodium vegetable broth
- 1 cup sliced carrots
- 2 red bell peppers, diced
- 1 medium sweet potato, peeled and diced
- 1 large onion, diced
- 2 tablespoons grated fresh ginger
- 1 tablespoon curry powder
- 1 tablespoon turmeric
- 4 garlic cloves, minced
- Freshly ground black pepper
- Pinch cayenne pepper (optional)
- 1½ cups frozen peas

Directions:
1. Put the tomatoes, chickpeas, coconut milk, cauliflower, broth, carrots, bell peppers, sweet potato, onion, ginger, curry powder, turmeric, garlic, pepper, and cayenne pepper (if using) in a 6-quart slow cooker and stir to combine. Cover and cook on low for 7 to 8 hours, until the vegetables are tender.
2. Before serving, stir in the peas and let stand until warmed through.
3. Serve over brown rice or grain of choice.

Nutrition Info:
- Per Serving: Calories: 277 ; Fat: 8 g ;Cholesterol: 0 mg ;Sodium: 178 mg

Chapter 6 Salads, Soups, And Side Dishes Recipes

Sautéed Kale With Blood Orange Dressing

Cooking Time: 8 Minutes
Ingredients:
- 2 blood oranges (1 halved, 1 peeled and segmented)
- 2 tablespoons olive oil, plus 1 teaspoon
- 1 teaspoon honey
- 1 bunch kale, stems removed and chopped
- ¼ cup chopped walnuts
- Freshly ground black pepper

Directions:
1. Squeeze 3 tablespoons of juice from the halved blood orange. In a small bowl, mix together the orange juice, 2 tablespoons of olive oil, and the honey. Set it aside.
2. In a medium skillet, heat the remaining 1 teaspoon of olive oil, add the chopped kale stems and centers and sauté for 3 to 4 minutes, or until softened.
3. Add the kale leaves to the skillet, pour half of the dressing over them, and sauté for 2 to 3 minutes, or until the leaves are wilted and tender. Add the orange segments and cook for 1 minute, or until warm. Remove from the heat and add the remaining dressing, tossing lightly to combine.
4. Serve the kale topped with the walnuts and seasoned with pepper.

Nutrition Info:
- Per Serving: Calories: 433 ; Fat: 26 g ;Cholesterol: 0 mg ;Sodium: 87 mg

Hearty Mashed Potatoes

Servings: 4
Cooking Time: 25 Min
Ingredients:
- 1½ pounds mini new potatoes
- 1 tablespoon extra-virgin olive oil
- 1 tablespoon unsalted butter
- ½ cup plain 2% Greek yogurt
- 1 tablespoon nutritional yeast (optional)
- ¼ teaspoon salt (optional)
- Freshly ground black pepper (optional)
- Snipped fresh chives, for garnish (optional)

Directions:
1. Put the potatoes in a large pot, and pour in just enough water to cover them. Bring the water to a boil over high heat, then turn the heat down, cover, and simmer until the tip of a sharp knife slides easily into a potato, about 18 minutes.
2. Drain the potatoes, reserving the cooking water. Put the potatoes back in the pot, and turn the heat down to low. Use a potato masher to mash the potatoes with the olive oil and butter, then the yogurt. Add the reserved cooking water, ½ cup at a time, until the potatoes are as creamy as you like.
3. Using a wooden spoon, mix in the nutritional yeast, salt, and pepper (if using).
4. Taste, and adjust the seasonings. Top with snipped fresh chives, if you like, and another grind of black pepper.

Nutrition Info:
- Per Serving: Calories: 214 ; Fat: 7 g ;Cholesterol: 11 mg ;Sodium: 168 mg

Lime Wild Rice

Servings: 4
Cooking Time: 45 Min
Ingredients:
- 2 tbsp coconut oil
- 1 medium brown onion, finely chopped
- 2 cups low-sodium vegetable stock
- 1 cup wild rice
- ¼ cup lime juice
- 1 lime, zested
- ½ tsp parsley, chopped

Directions:
1. In a large sized stockpot, add the coconut oil over medium heat until hot.
2. Add the chopped onions, and cook for 3 to 5 minutes, until softened.
3. Add the vegetable stock, wild rice, and lime juice, allow to boil.

4. Reduce the heat to a simmer. Cover the stockpot, and cook for 30 to 40 minutes, or according to the instructions on the packet. Once the liquid has been absorbed, remove from the heat, and allow to rest for 10 minutes.

5. Mix in the lime zest and chopped parsley, serve warm.

Nutrition Info:
- Per Serving: Calories: 246 ; Fat:8 g ;Cholesterol: 0mg ;Sodium: 3 mg

Middle Eastern Bulgur Pilaf

Servings: 4
Cooking Time: 30 Min
Ingredients:
- 2 tablespoons extra-virgin olive oil, divided
- 2 cups frozen sliced red bell peppers and onions
- 2 garlic cloves, minced
- 1 cup uncooked bulgur
- ½ cup sliced sun-dried tomatoes in oil
- 2¼ cups reduced-sodium vegetable broth
- 8 ounces fresh snap peas
- 2 tablespoons red wine vinegar
- ¼ teaspoon freshly ground black pepper
- ⅓ cup crumbled feta cheese

Directions:
1. Heat 1 tablespoon of oil in a large skillet over medium-high heat. When it is hot, add the peppers and onions. Cook, stirring occasionally, until the vegetables are thawed, then turn the heat down to medium and add the garlic.
2. Stir for about a minute, then add the bulgur, sun-dried tomatoes, and broth. Turn the heat back up to bring it to a boil, then turn it down again, cover, and simmer for 12 minutes (set a timer).
3. Meanwhile, trim and cut the snap peas into bite-size pieces. When the timer goes off, add them to the bulgur, then set the timer for another 5 minutes.
4. When the timer goes off again, stir in the red wine vinegar, black pepper, and remaining 1 tablespoon of olive oil. Top with the feta cheese.

Nutrition Info:
- Per Serving: Calories: 300 ; Fat: 12 g ;Cholesterol: 11 mg;Sodium: 246 mg

Butternut Soup

Servings: 4
Cooking Time: 10 Min
Ingredients:
- 3 cups vegetable stock, divided
- 7 oz soft tofu, drained
- 1 (15 oz) canned butternut squash puree
- 1 tbsp orange zest, (optional)
- ½ tsp ground cinnamon
- Himalayan pink salt
- Ground black pepper

Directions:
1. In a blender, add 1 cup vegetable stock and the drained soft tofu, blend until smooth.
2. In a large sized stockpot over high heat, add the tofu mixture, 2 cups vegetable stock, the butternut squash puree, orange zest (if using) and ground cinnamon. Allow to boil.
3. Reduce the heat to low, and cook for 10 minutes, until the flavors combine and heated through. Remove from the heat and season with Himalayan pink salt and ground black pepper to taste.
4. Divide into bowls and serve hot.

Nutrition Info:
- Per Serving: Calories: 68; Fat: 2 g ;Cholesterol: 0 mg ;Sodium: 48 mg

Orange And Avocado Green Salad

Servings: 4
Cooking Time: 25 Min
Ingredients:
- ¼ cup shelled pistachios
- 1 large orange
- 2 tablespoons extra-virgin olive oil
- 2 tablespoons plain yogurt
- 2 teaspoons freshly squeezed lemon juice (about ½ small lemon)
- 2 teaspoons pure maple syrup
- ¼ teaspoon kosher salt

- Freshly ground black pepper
- 1 head butter, green leaf, or red leaf lettuce, torn into bite-size pieces
- 1 avocado, peeled, pitted, and chopped

Directions:
1. Preheat the oven to 350°F.
2. Spread the pistachios on a rimmed baking sheet and transfer to the oven. Shake after 5 minutes, check after another 3 minutes, and take them out when they look golden and smell nutty, usually no more than 12 minutes total. Remove from the pan to cool. When cool, chop them roughly.
3. Cut the orange in half. Squeeze the juice from one half into a large bowl for the dressing. Add the olive oil, yogurt, lemon juice, maple syrup, salt, and a grind of pepper; mix well.
4. Peel the other half of the orange, then cut the flesh into bite-size pieces. Add the lettuce, orange pieces, avocado, and pistachios to the bowl with the dressing, and toss well.

Nutrition Info:
- Per Serving: Calories: 198 ; Fat: 16 g ;Cholesterol: 0 mg ;Sodium: 165 mg

Honey-Glazed Carrots

Servings: 4
Cooking Time: 2 Minutes
Ingredients:
- 1 cup water
- 1 pound carrots, sliced
- 1 tablespoon olive oil
- ⅛ teaspoon salt
- 1 tablespoon honey
- ¼ teaspoon dried rosemary

Directions:
1. Pour 1 cup of water into the Instant Pot and set the trivet in the center.
2. Cut a piece of aluminum foil to fit over the trivet and set it on the trivet. Place the carrots on top.
3. Lock the lid into place. Select Pressure Cook and cook on high pressure for 2 minutes. When the cooking is complete, quick release the pressure and remove the lid.
4. Carefully remove the carrots. Turn off the Instant Pot and drain the water from the inner pot.
5. Return the inner liner to the Instant Pot. Combine the oil, salt, honey, and rosemary in the pot. Select Sauté and heat for 1 to 2 minutes, until the oil starts to shimmer. Press Cancel.
6. Return the carrots to the Instant Pot and toss with the honey mixture until well coated. Serve.

Nutrition Info:
- Per Serving: Calories: 102 ; Fat: 4 g ;Cholesterol: 0 mg ;Sodium: 168 mg

Mediterranean Cucumber, Tomato, And Kalamata Olive Salad

Servings: 2
Ingredients:
- 1 medium English cucumber, quartered
- ½ cup cherry tomatoes, halved
- ½ red onion, diced
- 1 teaspoon extra-virgin olive oil
- 1½ tablespoons lemon juice
- ¼ cup low-sodium Kalamata olives, drained and quartered (about 8)
- ¼ teaspoon freshly ground black pepper

Directions:
1. In a large mixing bowl, combine the cucumber, cherry tomatoes, onion, olive oil, lemon juice, olives, and pepper. Mix well and serve. The salad can be stored in an airtight container in the refrigerator for up to 2 days.

Nutrition Info:
- Per Serving: Calories: 96 ; Fat: 7 g ;Cholesterol: 0 mg ;Sodium: 222 mg

Rosemary Sweetato Mash

Servings: 4
Cooking Time: 20 Min
Ingredients:
- ¼ cup water
- 2 large sweet potatoes, peeled and cut into chunks
- 1 ½ tbsp garlic, crushed
- 1 tsp olive oil
- ¼ cup plus 1 tsp unsweetened soymilk
- 2 rosemary sprigs, stem removed
- ¼ tsp ground black pepper

Directions:
1. Put the water in a steamer pot and place the steamer basket on top with the sweet potato chunks. Cover, and steam on medium heat for 10 to 12 minutes, until the sweet potatoes are fully cooked.
2. In the meantime, in a small sized stockpot over medium heat, add the crushed garlic and olive oil, cook for 5 to 7 minutes, until lightly browned.
3. Transfer the garlic and cooked sweet potatoes into a food processor. Add the soymilk, rosemary, and ground black pepper. Purée for 1 minute, until the potatoes are creamy, thick and has a chunky consistency. Serve warm.

Nutrition Info:
- Per Serving: Calories: 76 ; Fat: 2 g ;Cholesterol: 0mg ;Sodium: 43 mg

Spicy Bean Soup

Servings: 6
Cooking Time: 10 Min
Ingredients:
- 1½ cups reduced-sodium vegetable stock
- 1 (15 oz) can no-salt-added kidney beans, rinsed and drained
- 1 (15 oz) can no salt added whole kernel corn, drained and rinsed
- ½ cup fresh tomato salsa or store bought
- 1½ cups broccoli florets, chopped
- 1½ tsp lemon juice, divided
- 2 spring onions, thinly sliced, divided
- Dash hot sauce, divided

Directions:
1. In a large sized stockpot, add the vegetable stock, drained kidney beans, drained whole corn, and fresh salsa. Allow to boil over high heat.
2. Add the broccoli florets and cook for 2 to 4 minutes, remove the stockpot from the heat as soon as the broccoli is tender.
3. Divide the soup into bowls. To each serving, add ¼ tsp of lemon juice, a sprinkle of sliced spring onion, and a dash of hot sauce. Serve hot.

Nutrition Info:
- Per Serving: Calories: 166 ; Fat: 6 g ;Cholesterol: 16 mg ;Sodium: 245 mg

Roasted Sweet Potatoes

Servings: 4
Cooking Time: 30 Min
Ingredients:
- 2 large sweet potatoes, well scrubbed
- 2 tablespoons canola or sunflower oil
- ½ teaspoon garlic powder
- ½ teaspoon onion powder
- ½ teaspoon dried oregano
- ½ teaspoon paprika
- ¼ teaspoon kosher salt
- Freshly ground black pepper

Directions:
1. Preheat the oven to 425°F. Line two rimmed baking sheets with parchment paper.
2. Cut the sweet potatoes into ¾-inch chunks. Toss the potatoes with the oil and the garlic powder, onion powder, oregano, paprika, salt, and pepper in a large bowl. Divide the coated potato pieces between the prepared baking sheets, spreading them out in single layers and making sure they aren't crowded.
3. Cook for about 25 minutes, turning every 10 minutes or so.

Nutrition Info:
- Per Serving: Calories: 177 ; Fat: 7 g ;Cholesterol: 0 mg ;Sodium: 192 mg

Root Vegetable Stew

Servings: 6 To 8
Cooking Time: 6 To 8 Hours
Ingredients:
- 1 pound Yukon gold potatoes, diced
- 1 pound sweet potatoes, diced
- 1 pound parsnips, diced
- 1 pound carrots, diced
- 4 cups Savory Vegetable Broth (here)
- 3 cups diced butternut squash
- 2 medium beets, peeled and diced
- 2 medium onions, diced
- 1 (15-ounce) can chickpeas, drained and rinsed
- 4 garlic cloves, minced
- 2 bay leaves
- 2 teaspoons dried sage
- Freshly ground black pepper

Directions:
1. Combine all the ingredients in a 6-quart slow cooker. Cover and cook on low for 6 to 8 hours, until the vegetables are tender.
2. Remove and discard the bay leaves and serve hot.

Nutrition Info:
- Per Serving: Calories: 357 ; Fat: 0 g ;Cholesterol: 0 mg ;Sodium: 240 mg

Roasted Lentil Snack Mix

Servings: 4
Cooking Time: 25 Minutes
Ingredients:
- 1 cup dried red lentils
- 1 cup whole unsalted shelled pistachios
- ½ cup unsalted shelled sunflower seeds
- ½ cup dried cherries
- ½ cup dark chocolate chips

Directions:
1. In a bowl, cover the lentils with water, and soak for 1 hour. Drain.
2. Preheat the oven to 350°F.
3. Transfer the lentils to a clean kitchen towel, and dab gently. Set aside for about 10 minutes to dry.
4. Spread the lentils out on a large baking sheet.
5. Transfer the baking sheet to the oven, and bake, stirring once or twice, for 20 to 25 minutes, or until the lentils are crisp. Remove from the oven. Let cool to room temperature. Transfer to a large bowl.
6. Add the pistachios, sunflower seeds, cherries, and chocolate chips. Toss to combine.
7. Let cool, and store in an airtight container at room temperature for up to 1 month.

Nutrition Info:
- Per Serving: Calories: 629 ; Fat: 32 g ;Cholesterol: 0mg ;Sodium: 12mg

Brussels Sprouts And Pancetta

Servings: 4
Cooking Time: 25 Min
Ingredients:
- 1 pound Brussels sprouts, trimmed and halved
- 1 onion, diced
- ½ cup cubed pancetta
- 3 garlic cloves, minced
- 1 teaspoon balsamic vinegar
- ¼ cup slivered almonds
- ⅛ teaspoon salt
- Freshly ground black pepper

Directions:
1. Pour an inch or so of water into a medium pot, and bring to a boil over medium-high heat. Add the Brussels sprouts, cover, and cook for 6 minutes.
2. Meanwhile, in a large, heavy skillet, sauté the onion and pancetta until the onion is transparent, 3 to 4 minutes. Add the garlic, balsamic vinegar, and almonds. Cook for another minute, then slide them out of the pan and onto a plate.
3. Use a slotted spoon to transfer the Brussels sprouts to the same skillet, cut-sides down, and sauté over medium-high heat for 5 to 7 minutes. When they start to get crisp, add the onion mixture and mix thoroughly. Season with salt and pepper.

Nutrition Info:

- Per Serving: Calories: 208 ; Fat: 14 g ;Cholesterol: 16 mg ;Sodium: 472 mg

Umami Mushrooms

Servings: 2
Cooking Time: 15 Min
Ingredients:
- 8 ounces white button, cremini, or portobello mushrooms
- 2 tablespoons extra-virgin olive oil
- 1 tablespoon balsamic vinegar
- 2 teaspoons reduced-sodium tamari
- 1 garlic clove, minced

Directions:
1. Rinse the mushrooms, then pat them dry with a paper towel. Trim them only if the ends look tough, and cut them into thick slices.
2. Preheat a heavy skillet over medium-high heat. Add the oil to pan. When the oil is shimmering, add the mushrooms and toss to coat. Cook, stirring only occasionally, for 7 to 10 minutes, until any water released by the mushrooms has evaporated and they're golden brown. If they start to brown too quickly, turn down the heat.
3. Turn the heat down to medium-low. Add the balsamic vinegar and tamari, and sauté until dry. Add the garlic, and sauté for 1 minute.

Nutrition Info:
- Per Serving: Calories: 157 ; Fat: 14 g ;Cholesterol: 0 mg;Sodium: 200 mg

Quinoa Spinach Power Salad

Cooking Time: 10 Minutes
Ingredients:
- 2 cups water
- ½ cup uncooked quinoa, rinsed and drained
- 2 cups finely chopped spinach
- 1 cup sugar snap peas
- ¾ cup diced tomato
- ½ cup diced cucumbers
- ¼ cup sliced almonds
- 1½ tablespoons freshly squeezed lemon juice
- 1½ tablespoons olive oil
- ¼ teaspoon salt
- ¼ teaspoon freshly ground black pepper

Directions:
1. Bring the water to a boil in a medium saucepan. Add the quinoa and continue to boil until the quinoa is tender, about 10 minutes.
2. Drain the quinoa and let it cool.
3. In a large bowl, combine the spinach, peas, tomato, cucumber, almonds, and cooled quinoa.
4. In a small bowl, whisk together the lemon juice, olive oil, salt, and pepper. Drizzle over the salad and toss to coat.
5. Divide between two serving bowls and enjoy.

Nutrition Info:
- Per Serving: Calories: 322 ; Fat:18 g ;Cholesterol: 0mg ;Sodium: 325 mg

Baked Beet Salad

Servings: 4
Cooking Time: 35 Minutes
Ingredients:
- 1 bunch (3 or 4 medium) beets
- 1 (8-ounce) bag arugula
- ¼ cup Balsamic Vinaigrette
- ¼ cup chopped almonds
- ¼ cup crumbled goat cheese

Directions:
1. Preheat the oven to 350°F.
2. Wash the beets well. Wrap them in aluminum foil.
3. Transfer the beets to the oven, and bake for 25 to 35 minutes, depending on the size of the beets, or until easily pierced with a fork. Remove from the oven. Let cool until easy to handle.
4. Using your hands, slide the skins off the beets, and discard. Cut the beets into wedges.
5. Put the beets in a large bowl with the arugula.
6. Drizzle the vinaigrette over the beets, and toss gently.
7. Serve the salad topped with the almonds and cheese.

Nutrition Info:
- Per Serving: Calories: 197 ; Fat: 14 g ;Cholesterol: 0mg ;Sodium: 171 mg

Cauliflower Steak With Arugula-Basil Pesto

Servings: 2
Cooking Time: 20 Minutes
Ingredients:
- 2 teaspoons avocado oil
- 1 tablespoon lemon juice
- 1 teaspoon garlic powder
- ½ head cauliflower, sliced lengthwise into 1-inch-thick "steaks"
- 2 tablespoons Arugula-Basil Pesto

Directions:
1. Preheat the oven to 400°F. Line a baking sheet with parchment paper.
2. In a small mixing bowl, combine the oil, lemon juice, and garlic powder. Evenly brush the dressing over each side of the cauliflower steaks. Transfer the steaks to the prepared baking sheet.
3. Roast for 10 minutes, flip, and roast for an additional 10 minutes, until the cauliflower is fork-tender and the edges are lightly browned.
4. Top the steaks with the pesto. Serve immediately.

Nutrition Info:
- Per Serving: Calories:185 ; Fat: 15 g ;Cholesterol: 0mg ;Sodium: 50 mg

Arugula Salad With Fennel

Servings: 4
Cooking Time: 10 Minutes
Ingredients:
- 8 cups baby arugula
- 1 fennel bulb, cored and thinly sliced
- 3 tablespoons Lemon Vinaigrette
- ¼ cup chopped hazelnuts

Directions:
1. In a large bowl, toss together the arugula and fennel.
2. Drizzle with the vinaigrette, and toss again.
3. Serve the salad topped with the hazelnuts.

Nutrition Info:
- Per Serving: Calories: 163 ; Fat: 14 g ;Cholesterol: 0mg ;Sodium: 152 mg

Quick Kale Caesar Salad

Servings: 4
Cooking Time: 15 Min
Ingredients:
- For the dressing
- 2 tablespoons extra-virgin olive oil, plus more if needed
- 2 tablespoons mayonnaise
- 1 tablespoon freshly squeezed lemon juice
- 1 tablespoon red wine vinegar
- 1 teaspoon Dijon mustard
- 1 small garlic clove, minced
- ⅛ teaspoon kosher salt
- For the salad
- 1 (5-ounce) package prewashed baby kale
- 2 tablespoons grated Parmesan cheese
- ¼ cup Parmesan crisps (optional)

Directions:
1. In a large bowl, whisk together the oil, mayonnaise, lemon juice, vinegar, mustard, garlic, and salt.
2. Add the kale and toss well with the dressing, then add the Parmesan cheese and toss again. If needed, add a bit more oil, so it's not dry.
3. Top with Parmesan crisps (if using).

Nutrition Info:
- Per Serving: Calories: 156 ; Fat: 14 g ;Cholesterol: 8 mg ;Sodium: 242 mg

Vegetable Chips With Rosemary Salt

Servings: 4
Cooking Time: 50 Minutes
Ingredients:
- Olive oil cooking spray
- 2 medium beets, peeled and sliced
- 1 medium zucchini, sliced
- 1 medium sweet potato, sliced
- 1 small rutabaga, peeled and sliced
- ½ teaspoon salt, plus more to sweat the vegetables
- ¼ teaspoon dried rosemary

Directions:
1. Preheat the oven to 300°F. Spray a baking sheet with cooking spray. Line a plate with paper towels.
2. Lay the beets, zucchini, sweet potato, and rutabaga in a single layer on a paper towel. Lightly salt, and let sit for 10 minutes.
3. Cover the vegetables with another paper towel, and blot away any moisture on top.
4. Arrange the vegetables on the prepared baking sheet, and spray with cooking spray.
5. Transfer the baking sheet to the oven, and cook for 30 to 40 minutes, or until the vegetables have browned.
6. Flip the vegetables, and cook for 10 minutes, or until crisped. Remove from the oven. Transfer to the prepared plate to drain any excess oil.
7. In a small bowl, mix together the salt and rosemary.
8. Lightly season the chips with the rosemary salt.

Nutrition Info:
- Per Serving: Calories: 72 ; Fat: 0 g ;Cholesterol: 0mg ;Sodium: 350 mg

Lemon-Roasted Asparagus

Servings: 2
Cooking Time: 15 Minutes
Ingredients:
- 1 bunch asparagus, trimmed 1 inch from the bottom (20 or 30 spears)
- 2 teaspoons avocado oil
- 2 teaspoons lemon zest
- 2 tablespoons lemon juice
- 2 garlic cloves, minced
- ½ teaspoon freshly ground black pepper

Directions:
1. Preheat the oven to 425°F. Line a baking sheet with parchment paper and lay out the asparagus.
2. Mix the oil, lemon zest, lemon juice, garlic, and pepper and toss with the asparagus until well coated.
3. Bake for 12 to 15 minutes, until the asparagus is fork-tender and the tops are crispy. This dish can be stored in an airtight container for up to 5 days, but is best served warm.

Nutrition Info:
- Per Serving: Calories: 90 ; Fat: 5 g ;Cholesterol: 0mg ;Sodium: 9 mg

Lemon Chicken Orzo Soup

Servings: 6
Cooking Time: 7 To 8 Hours
Ingredients:
- 1 pound boneless, skinless chicken breasts
- 4 cups Savory Vegetable Broth (here) or low-sodium vegetable broth
- 2 cups Chicken Stock (here) or low-sodium chicken broth
- 2 large carrots, sliced
- 2 celery stalks, finely chopped
- 6 garlic cloves, minced
- 1 teaspoon dried basil
- 1 teaspoon Italian seasoning
- 2 bay leaves
- Juice of 1 lemon
- ½ cup chopped fresh parsley
- 8 ounces orzo (wholewheat is ideal)
- Freshly ground black pepper

Directions:
1. Place the chicken, vegetable broth, chicken stock, carrots, celery, garlic, basil, Italian seasoning, and bay leaves in a 6-quart slow cooker. Cover and cook on low for 7 to 8 hours.
2. About 30 minutes prior to serving, remove discard the bay leaves. Use two forks to shred the chicken. Stir in the lemon juice, parsley, orzo, and pepper. Cook for 30 minutes,

until the orzo is tender, stirring every 10 minutes or so because the orzo may stick to the bottom of the slow cooker.
3. Serve immediately.

Nutrition Info:
- Per Serving: Calories: 259 ; Fat: 2 g ;Cholesterol: 43 mg ;Sodium: 179 mg

Zucchini Noodles

Servings: 4
Cooking Time: 5 Minutes
Ingredients:
- 2 tablespoons extra-virgin olive oil
- 2 garlic cloves, minced
- 2 medium zucchini, spiralized
- ½ teaspoon salt
- ½ teaspoon freshly ground black pepper
- ½ cup chopped fresh parsley
- ¼ cup shredded Parmesan cheese

Directions:
1. In a large skillet, heat the oil over medium-high heat.
2. Add the garlic, and cook for about 30 seconds, or until fragrant.
3. Add the zucchini, salt, and pepper. Cook for 2 to 3 minutes, or until the noodles are just barely al dente. Remove from the heat.
4. Serve the noodles topped with the parsley and cheese.

Nutrition Info:
- Per Serving: Calories: 108 ; Fat: 9 g ;Cholesterol: 0mg ;Sodium: 416 mg

Minestrone Soup

Servings: 6 To 8
Cooking Time: 7 To 8 Hours
Ingredients:
- 6 cups Savory Vegetable Broth (here) or low-sodium vegetable broth
- 1 (28-ounce) can no-salt-added diced tomatoes
- 1 (14.5-ounce) can white kidney beans, drained and rinsed
- 1 (14.5-ounce) can red kidney beans, drained and rinsed
- 2 large onions, chopped
- 3 celery stalks, chopped
- 2 carrots, chopped
- 1 medium zucchini, diced
- 1½ cups fresh green beans, trimmed and cut into ½-inch pieces
- 1 cup chopped fresh spinach
- ½ cup hulled barley
- 4 garlic cloves, minced
- 1 tablespoon chopped fresh parsley
- Freshly ground black pepper

Directions:
1. Combine all the ingredients in a 6-quart slow cooker. Cover and cook on low for 7 to 8 hours.
2. Serve warm.

Nutrition Info:
- Per Serving: Calories: 254 ; Fat: 0 g ;Cholesterol: 0 mg ;Sodium: 188 mg

Brussel Sprouts Hummus

Servings: 8
Cooking Time: 15 Min
Ingredients:
- 1 (15 oz) can garbanzo beans, drained and rinsed
- ¼ cup unsalted cashew butter
- 1 tbsp garlic, crushed
- 3 tbsp lemon juice
- 3 tbsp avocado oil
- 1 cup Brussel Sprouts, chopped
- 3 tbsp basil, chopped
- 4 tbsp water
- Ground black pepper

Directions:
1. In a blender, add the garbanzo beans, cashew butter, crushed garlic, lemon juice, avocado oil, Brussel sprouts, chopped basil, water, and ground black pepper, blend until smooth.

2. Enjoy immediately or serve on a grilled chicken breast.

Nutrition Info:
- Per Serving: Calories: 242 ; Fat: 16 g ;Cholesterol: 0mg ;Sodium: 51 mg

Granny Smith Salad

Servings: 2
Cooking Time: 10 Min
Ingredients:
- 1 tbsp organic apple cider vinegar
- 1 tbsp avocado oil
- 2 tsp organic honey
- 4 cups red cabbage, cut into bite-size pieces
- 2 Granny Smith apples, core removed and cut into thin slices
- Ground black pepper

Directions:
1. In a large sized mixing bowl, add the apple cider vinegar, avocado oil, and organic honey, mix to combine.
2. In the same mixing bowl, add the cut cabbage and sliced apples and mix to combine.
3. Season with ground black pepper to taste. Serve immediately.

Nutrition Info:
- Per Serving: Calories: 176 ; Fat: 7 g ;Cholesterol: 0mg ;Sodium: 34mg

Sage-Roasted Baby Carrots

Cooking Time: 20 Minutes
Ingredients:
- 1 pound baby carrots
- 2 tablespoons chopped fresh sage
- 1 tablespoon orange zest
- 1 tablespoon olive oil
- Juice of ½ lemon

Directions:
1. Preheat the oven to 425°F and line a baking sheet with parchment paper.
2. In a medium bowl, combine the carrots, sage, orange zest, and olive oil.
3. Spread the carrots in a single layer on the prepared baking sheet and roast for about 20 minutes, or until soft and slightly browned.
4. Drizzle the lemon juice over the carrots before serving.

Nutrition Info:
- Per Serving: Calories: 149 ; Fat: 7 g ;Cholesterol: 0 mg ;Sodium: 177 mg

Roasted Peppers And Zucchini

Servings: 4
Cooking Time: 30 Minutes
Ingredients:
- 2 small zucchini, sliced
- 2 bell peppers, cored and cut into 1-inch pieces
- 1 red onion, cut into 1-inch pieces
- 2 tablespoons extra-virgin olive oil
- 1 tablespoon freshly squeezed lemon juice
- 1 teaspoon Italian seasoning
- Salt
- Freshly ground black pepper

Directions:
1. Preheat the oven to 425°F.
2. On a baking sheet, combine the zucchini, bell peppers, and onion.
3. Drizzle with the oil, lemon juice, and Italian seasoning. Toss to coat. Season with salt and pepper. Stir to combine.
4. Spread the vegetables in an even layer.
5. Transfer the baking sheet to the oven, and roast, tossing once about halfway through, for 30 minutes, or until the vegetables are tender and browned on the edges. Remove from the oven. Serve warm.

Nutrition Info:
- Per Serving: Calories: 107 ; Fat: 7 g ;Cholesterol: 0mg ;Sodium: 47 mg

Polenta Cakes

Servings: 4
Cooking Time: 40 Minutes
Ingredients:
- 5 cups water
- 1 cup fine cornmeal
- 1 teaspoon garlic powder
- ¼ teaspoon salt
- Olive oil cooking spray
- 2 tablespoons extra-virgin olive oil, divided

Directions:
1. In a large saucepan, bring the water to a rolling boil over high heat.
2. While whisking, slowly pour the cornmeal into the water, and continue whisking until well combined.
3. Whisk in the garlic powder and salt.
4. Reduce the heat to a simmer. Cook, stirring regularly, for 25 to 30 minutes, or until the cornmeal has thickened. Remove from the heat.
5. Meanwhile, spray a 9-by-13-inch baking dish with cooking spray. Line with parchment paper.
6. Pour the mixture into the prepared dish. Using a spoon, smooth the surface. Refrigerate for at least 2 hours, or until solid.
7. Lift the parchment paper from the dish. Cut the polenta into 12 pieces, or use a cookie cutter to create circular cakes if desired.
8. In a large skillet, heat the oil over medium-high heat.
9. Working in batches, add the polenta cakes, and cook for 2 to 3 minutes per side, or until browned. Remove from the heat.

Nutrition Info:
- Per Serving: Calories: 173 ; Fat: 8 g ;Cholesterol: 0mg ;Sodium: 157 mg

Tempeh Taco Salad With Chile-Lime Glaze

Servings: 2
Cooking Time: 5 Minutes
Ingredients:
- 1 teaspoon avocado oil
- ¼ red onion, diced (about ¼ cup diced)
- 1 garlic clove, minced
- ½ bar of tempeh (4 ounces), crumbled with a fork
- 2 teaspoons tomato paste, double-concentrated
- ¼ cup water
- ¼ teaspoon Barbeque Seasoning Rub Blend
- 1 head romaine lettuce, chopped
- 1 cup tomatoes, diced
- 1 medium cucumber, quartered
- ¼ avocado, sliced
- 2 tablespoons Chile-Lime Glaze

Directions:
1. In a medium pan, heat the oil over medium-low heat and add the onion and garlic. Sauté for about 1 minute, until the onion becomes translucent.
2. Add the tempeh, tomato paste, water, and barbeque seasoning and stir constantly until lightly browned, about 3 minutes.
3. Divide the romaine lettuce, tomatoes, cucumber, tempeh mixture, and avocado into two serving bowls. Drizzle with the glaze. The tempeh mixture can be made 2 to 3 days in advance and kept in the refrigerator.

Nutrition Info:
- Per Serving: Calories: 225 ; Fat: 11 g ;Cholesterol: 0 mg ;Sodium: 11 mg

African Peanut Stew

Servings: 6 To 8
Cooking Time: 7 To 8 Hours
Ingredients:
- 4 cups Chicken Stock (here) or low-sodium chicken broth
- 1 (14.5-ounce) can no-salt-added diced tomatoes
- ½ cup chunky peanut butter
- 1 tablespoon ground cumin
- 1 teaspoon ground coriander
- ¼ teaspoon salt
- 3 tablespoons minced fresh ginger
- 2 pounds boneless, skinless chicken breasts, cut into 1-inch pieces
- 1 large sweet potato (about 1 pound), peeled and cubed
- 2 medium zucchini (1 pound), cubed
- 1 (14.5-ounce) can chickpeas, drained and rinsed

- ½ cup chopped roasted unsalted peanuts
- ¼ cup chopped cilantro

Directions:
1. In a blender or food processor, add the stock, tomatoes, peanut butter, cumin, coriander, and salt and blend until thick and pasty.
2. In a 6-quart slow cooker, combine the ginger, chicken, sweet potato, zucchini, and chickpeas. Pour the sauce over the chicken and vegetables. Cover and cook on low for 7 to 8 hours. The finished stew should reach a temperature of 165°F.
3. Garnish the finished stew with the chopped peanuts and cilantro.

Nutrition Info:
- Per Serving: Calories: 476 ; Fat: 21 g ;Cholesterol: 87 mg ;Sodium: 345 mg

Warm Balsamic Beet Salad With Sunflower Seeds

Servings: 2
Cooking Time: 15 Minutes
Ingredients:
- 2 teaspoons avocado oil
- 3 medium whole beets, including greens and roots, chopped, divided
- 1 tablespoon balsamic vinegar
- 1 tablespoon sunflower seeds

Directions:
1. In a medium pot, heat the oil over medium heat for about 2 minutes.
2. Add the beet roots and cook, covered, for 5 to 7 minutes, until they are fork-tender but not soft.
3. Add the beet greens to the pan and cook for an additional 5 to 7 minutes, uncovered, until the beets are tender and the greens are wilted.
4. In a large mixing bowl, combine balsamic vinegar, sunflower seeds, and the beet mixture and serve or store in an airtight container in the refrigerator for up to 3 days.

Nutrition Info:
- Per Serving: Calories: 111 ; Fat: 5g ;Cholesterol: 0 mg ;Sodium: 141 mg

Garden Vegetable Stew With Toasted Cashews

Cooking Time: 30 Minutes
Ingredients:
- 1 tablespoon olive oil, plus 2 teaspoons, divided
- 1 small cayenne pepper, seeded and minced
- ½ cup chopped onion
- ½ cup chopped red bell pepper
- 2 garlic cloves, minced
- 2 teaspoons low-sodium tamari sauce
- 2 cups water
- ½ cup thinly sliced carrots
- ½ cup diced fresh tomato
- 1 cup chopped eggplant
- 1 cup sliced green beans
- ¾ cup fresh corn kernels
- ½ cup raw cashews
- ½ cup thinly sliced shallots
- 2 cups chopped Swiss chard
- Salt
- Freshly ground black pepper

Directions:
1. Heat 1 tablespoon of olive oil in a large saucepan over medium heat. Add the cayenne pepper, onion, bell pepper, and garlic and cook for about 2 minutes, or until very fragrant and the onion has softened slightly.
2. Add the tamari and water. Bring to a boil, then add the carrots. Decrease the heat and simmer for 3 minutes.
3. Add the tomato and eggplant and cook for 1 minute. Add the green beans and corn and cook for 2 to 3 more minutes. Decrease the heat to low.
4. Meanwhile, in a small sauté pan, heat 1 teaspoon of olive oil over medium-low heat. Add the cashews to the pan and toast them for 4 to 5 minutes, or until they brown on all sides. Transfer them to a small plate.
5. Return the sauté pan to the heat and add the remaining 1 teaspoon of olive oil. Add the shallots to the pan and stir for 10 to 15 minutes, or until they turn a deep brown and crisp in some areas. Set them aside.

6. Bring the pot of stew back to a boil and add the Swiss chard. Cook until the greens wilt, about 1 minute. Season with salt and pepper.
7. Ladle the stew into serving bowls, top each bowl with toasted cashews and some shallots, and serve.

Nutrition Info:
- Per Serving: Calories: 457 ; Fat: 29 g ;Cholesterol: 0 mg ;Sodium: 500 mg

Moroccan Spiced Red Lentil And Millet Stew

Cooking Time: 50 Minutes
Ingredients:
- ½ tablespoon olive oil
- ½ cup finely chopped onion
- 3 cups low-sodium vegetable broth
- ⅓ cup dry millet
- 1 cup dried lentils, rinsed
- 1 celery stalk, chopped
- ½ cup finely chopped red bell pepper
- 2 tablespoons tomato paste
- ⅛ teaspoon cayenne pepper
- 1 teaspoon ground coriander
- ½ teaspoon ground cumin
- ¼ teaspoon ground cinnamon
- ½ cup chopped dried apricots
- Salt

Directions:
1. Heat the olive oil in a 3-quart stockpot or saucepan over medium heat. Add the onion and cook stirring frequently, until the onion is fragrant, about 6 minutes.
2. Add the broth, millet, and lentils. Bring the mixture to a boil.
3. Add the celery, bell pepper, tomato paste, cayenne, coriander, cumin, cinnamon, dried apricots, and salt to taste. Turn down the heat, cover and let simmer for 35 to 45 minutes, or until the lentils and millet are tender.
4. Serve hot.

Nutrition Info:
- Per Serving: Calories: 573 ; Fat: 7 g ;Cholesterol: 0 mg ;Sodium: 429 mg

Roasted Eggplant With Tahini-Garlic Dressing

Servings: 2
Cooking Time: 20 Minutes
Ingredients:
- ¼ teaspoon smoked paprika
- 1 teaspoon avocado oil
- 2 small eggplants, cut into bite-size pieces
- ¼ cup Tahini-Garlic Dressing

Directions:
1. Preheat the oven to 425°F. Line a baking sheet with parchment paper.
2. Evenly coat the eggplant with the paprika and oil. Spread the eggplant on the prepared baking sheet.
3. Bake for 10 minutes, then flip and stir the eggplant pieces and bake for another 10 minutes, until the eggplant is fork-tender and some pieces are caramelized.
4. Add the eggplant to the dressing and toss to coat. Divide into appropriate portions and serve, or store in the refrigerator for 3 to 4 days.

Nutrition Info:
- Per Serving: Calories: 264 ; Fat: 15 g ;Cholesterol: 0mg ;Sodium: 70 mg

Beet And Fennel Salad

Servings: 4
Cooking Time: 20 Minutes
Ingredients:
- 1½ cups water
- 2 large beets, scrubbed and dried
- Nonstick cooking spray
- 1 small fennel bulb, sliced (about 1 cup)
- 1 tablespoon balsamic vinegar
- 1 tablespoon honey
- Juice of ½ lemon
- 2 cups baby arugula

- 2 ounces feta cheese, crumbled
- Freshly ground black pepper (optional)

Directions:
1. Pour 1½ cups of water into the Instant Pot and set the trivet in the center.
2. Lightly coat each beet with nonstick spray. Wrap each tightly in aluminum foil and place on the trivet.
3. Lock the lid into place. Select Pressure Cook and cook on high pressure for 20 minutes. When the cooking is complete, allow the pressure to release naturally for 10 minutes, then quick release any remaining pressure and remove the lid.
4. Carefully remove the beets from the pot and let cool for 20 minutes. Unwrap each beet, using the foil and the pressure of your fingertips to peel the skin away and reveal the shiny beet flesh.
5. Chop the beets into ½-inch cubes (you should have about 1½ cups) and place in a medium bowl. Add the fennel, vinegar, honey, and lemon juice and toss until completed coated. Gently fold in the arugula and top with the feta. Season with pepper (if using)
6. Divide evenly among four small plates and serve.

Nutrition Info:
- Per Serving: Calories: 147 ; Fat: 9.5 g ;Cholesterol: 13 mg ;Sodium: 226 mg

Roasted Summer Squash Farro Salad

Servings: 2
Cooking Time: 20 Minutes
Ingredients:
- 1 cup water
- ¼ cup farro
- 1 medium yellow squash, cut into ½-inch-thick pieces
- 1 medium green zucchini, cut into ½-inch-thick pieces
- 1 teaspoon dried basil
- ½ teaspoon freshly ground black pepper
- 2 tablespoons Arugula-Basil Pesto

Directions:
1. Preheat the oven to 450°F. Line a baking sheet with parchment paper.
2. In a small saucepan, bring the water to a boil and add the farro. Reduce the heat, cover, and bring to a simmer for 20 minutes. Once the water has soaked into the farro, fluff it with a fork.
3. In the meantime, place the squash, zucchini, basil, and pepper on the baking sheet and coat with the spice mixture. Bake for 10 minutes, then flip and stir the pieces and bake for an additional 5 minutes.
4. In a medium mixing bowl, combine the farro, vegetables, and pesto. Serve immediately or chilled. The salad can be stored in an airtight container in the refrigerator for up to 4 days.

Nutrition Info:
- Per Serving: Calories: 225 ; Fat: 11 g ;Cholesterol: 0 mg ;Sodium: 11 mg

Simple Roasted Peppers

Servings: 4
Cooking Time: 25 Min
Ingredients:
- 4 red, yellow, and orange bell peppers, seeded and sliced
- 1 red onion, sliced (optional)
- 2 tablespoons canola or sunflower oil
- ¼ teaspoon salt (optional)
- Freshly ground black pepper (optional)

Directions:
1. Preheat the oven to 400°F.
2. Combine the peppers and onion (if using) in a large bowl. Add the oil and toss gently.
3. Spread out the peppers on one or two rimmed baking sheets. Make sure they're not too crowded, or they'll steam instead of roast.
4. Roast the peppers for 15 minutes, then toss them and roast for 5 minutes more, until they're done to your liking. Charred spots are fine—even desirable. Season with salt and pepper, if you want.

Nutrition Info:
- Per Serving: Calories: 110 ; Fat: 7 g ;Cholesterol: 0 mg ;Sodium: 151 mg

Mixed Veg Crisps

Servings: 4
Cooking Time: 50 Min

Ingredients:
- Aluminum foil
- 2 large beets, peeled and thinly sliced
- 1 medium courgette, thinly sliced
- 1 large sweet potato, thinly sliced
- 1 large turnips, peeled and thinly sliced
- ½ tsp Himalayan pink salt, plus more to sweat the vegetables
- Cooking spray
- ¼ tsp dried rosemary

Directions:

1. Heat the oven to 300°F gas mark 2. Line a baking sheet with aluminum foil.
2. Lay the sliced beets, sliced courgettes, sliced sweet potatoes, and sliced turnips in a single layer on several paper towels. Season lightly with Himalayan pink salt and allow to sit for 10 minutes.
3. Place more paper towel over the vegetables and blot the moisture away.
4. Place the sliced vegetables on the baking sheet and spray with cooking spray.
5. Transfer the baking sheet to the oven and roast for 30 to 40 minutes, or until the vegetables have browned.
6. Turn the vegetable slices over and cook for 10 minutes, until crispy. Remove from oven and transfer to a paper towel lined plate to drain excess oil.
7. In a small sized mixing bowl, add the Himalayan pink salt and dried rosemary, mix to combine.
8. Season the vegetable chips with the rosemary and salt seasoning.

Nutrition Info:
- Per Serving: Calories: 72 ; Fat: 0g ;Cholesterol: 0mg ;Sodium: 350mg

Chapter 7 Sauces, Staples, And Sweet Treats Recipes

Mushroom And Thyme Gravy

Servings: 4
Cooking Time: 30 Min
Ingredients:
- 1 tablespoon Better Butter or 1½ teaspoons unsalted butter plus 1½ teaspoons extra-virgin olive oil
- ½ onion, finely chopped
- 2 garlic cloves, minced
- 8 ounces sliced mushrooms
- ¼ teaspoon salt
- ¼ teaspoon freshly ground black pepper
- 2 tablespoons all-purpose flour
- 1 cup reduced-sodium beef broth
- 1 tablespoon chopped fresh thyme
- 1 tablespoon half-and-half (optional)

Directions:
1. Heat the Better Butter in a large skillet over medium heat. When it starts to froth, add the onion, garlic, mushrooms, salt, and pepper. Turn the heat up to medium-high, and cook the mushrooms until browned, about 10 minutes.
2. Stir in the flour and cook, stirring frequently, for about 5 minutes.
3. Add the broth slowly, stirring briskly to incorporate. When it starts to boil, turn the heat down to medium-low. Add the thyme. Simmer for another 10 minutes or so, adding more broth if it gets too thick. Stir in the half-and-half (if using). Taste, and adjust the seasonings.

Nutrition Info:
- Per Serving: Calories: 72 ; Fat: 4 g ;Cholesterol: 5 mg ;Sodium: 247 mg

Cinnamon-Vanilla Custard

Servings: 4
Cooking Time: 10 Minutes
Ingredients:
- Nonstick cooking spray
- 3 medium eggs, lightly whisked
- 1½ cups unsweetened oat milk
- 1 teaspoon vanilla extract
- 1 teaspoon ground cinnamon, divided
- 2 tablespoons brown sugar or granulated sugar
- 1½ cups water

Directions:
1. Lightly coat a 6-inch round cake pan with nonstick spray.
2. In a medium bowl, combine the eggs, milk, vanilla, ½ teaspoon of cinnamon, and the sugar. Whisk until well combined. Pour into the prepared cake pan and loosely cover with aluminum foil.
3. Pour 1½ cups of water into the Instant Pot and set the trivet in the center. Place the cake pan on the trivet.
4. Lock the lid into place. Select Pressure Cook and cook on high pressure for 7 minutes. Quick release the pressure. Remove the foil and give the custard a good whisk. Return the foil, place the pan back in the Instant Pot, lock the lid, and cook for another 3 minutes on high pressure. When the cooking is complete, quick release the pressure and remove the lid.
5. Remove the cake pan and the foil and let cool for 15 minutes.
6. Dust with the remaining ½ teaspoon of cinnamon. For best results, refrigerate for another 20 minutes until cool before serving.

Nutrition Info:
- Per Serving: Calories: 124 ; Fat: 6 g ;Cholesterol: 123 mg ;Sodium: 88 mg

Vanilla Pear Crisp

Servings: 6
Cooking Time: 4 To 5 Hours
Ingredients:
- 5 pears, chopped (peeling is optional)
- 1 apple, chopped (peeling is optional)
- ½ cup finely chopped dried figs
- ⅓ cup loosely packed brown sugar
- 2 teaspoons ground cinnamon
- 2 teaspoons vanilla extract
- 1 teaspoon ground nutmeg

- ½ cup whole-wheat flour, divided
- 1 cup old-fashioned oats
- ¼ cup honey
- 2 tablespoons coconut oil

Directions:
1. Put the pears, apple, and figs in a 6-quart slow cooker.
2. In a small bowl, combine the brown sugar, cinnamon, vanilla, nutmeg, and ¼ cup of flour. Pour this over the fruit and stir to combine.
3. In the same small bowl, combine the oats, remaining ¼ cup of flour, honey, and coconut oil. Spread this mixture on top of the fruit.
4. Cover and cook on low for 4 to 5 hours, until the fruit is soft.
5. Serve warm.

Nutrition Info:
- Per Serving: Calories: 305 ; Fat: 6 g ;Cholesterol: 0 mg ;Sodium: 4 mg

Sesame-Garlic Edamame

Servings: 4
Cooking Time: 10 Min
Ingredients:
- 1 (14-ounce) package frozen edamame in their shells
- 1 tablespoon canola or sunflower oil
- 1 tablespoon toasted sesame oil
- 3 garlic cloves, minced
- ½ teaspoon kosher salt
- ¼ teaspoon red pepper flakes (or more)

Directions:
1. Bring a large pot of water to a boil over high heat. Add the edamame, and cook just long enough to warm them up, 2 to 3 minutes.
2. Meanwhile, heat the canola oil, sesame oil, garlic, salt, and red pepper flakes in a large skillet over medium heat for 1 to 2 minutes, then remove the pan from the heat.
3. Drain the edamame and add them to the skillet, tossing to combine.

Nutrition Info:
- Per Serving: Calories: 173 ; Fat: 12 g ;Cholesterol: 0mg ;Sodium: 246mg

Fruit-Infused Sparkling Water

Servings: 2
Cooking Time: 5 Min
Ingredients:
- 1 (32-ounce/1 liter) bottle low-sodium club soda or sparkling water
- 3 orange segments, halved
- 5 raspberries, halved

Directions:
1. In a pitcher, combine the club soda and fruit.
2. Drink right away, or prepare in advance for more intense flavor.

Nutrition Info:
- Per Serving: Calories: 6 ; Fat: 0 g ;Cholesterol: 0 mg ;Sodium: 38 mg

Cheesy Kale Chips

Servings: 4
Cooking Time: 15 Minutes
Ingredients:
- 4 tablespoons unsalted tahini
- 4 heaping tablespoons nutritional yeast
- ½ teaspoon garlic powder
- ½ cup water
- 1 large bunch of kale, cut into 2-inch chunks (about 5 tightly packed cups)

Directions:
1. Preheat the oven to 400°F. Line a baking sheet with parchment paper.
2. In a large mixing bowl, combine the tahini, nutritional yeast, garlic powder, and water. The consistency should be runny enough to spread evenly over the kale.
3. Add the kale to the tahini mixture, thinly coating each kale piece, avoiding any clumpy chunks of sauce. Transfer

the dipped kale to the prepared baking sheet and spread so that the pieces don't touch.
4. Bake for 10 to 15 minutes, until the edges become slightly browned and the kale turns into a crispy chip. Serve alongside your favorite main dish or enjoy as a crunchy snack. Store in a large container for up to 3 days; the crispiness starts to fade in 24 hours.

Nutrition Info:
- Per Serving: Calories: 130 ; Fat: 9 g ;Cholesterol: 0 mg ;Sodium: 34 mg

Broiled Mango

Cooking Time: 10 Minutes
Ingredients:
- 1 mango, peeled, seeded, and sliced
- 1 lime, cut into wedges

Directions:
1. Position the rack in the upper third of the oven and preheat the broiler. Line a broiler pan with aluminum foil.
2. Arrange the mango slices in a single layer in the prepared pan. Broil for 8 to 10 minutes, or until browned in spots. Transfer to two plates, squeeze lime wedges over the broiled mango, and serve.

Nutrition Info:
- Per Serving: Calories: 101 ; Fat: 1 g ;Cholesterol: 0 mg ;Sodium: 2 mg

Zesty Carrot Tomato Sauce

Servings: 4
Cooking Time: 6 Minutes
Ingredients:
- 2 teaspoons olive oil
- ½ medium yellow onion, chopped
- 1 large red or orange bell pepper, sliced
- 2 garlic cloves, minced
- 2 medium carrots, chopped
- 1 (14.5-ounce) can low-sodium crushed tomatoes
- 1 (14-ounce) can diced fire-roasted tomatoes
- 2 teaspoons low-sodium soy sauce
- 1 tablespoon Italian seasoning

Directions:
1. Select Sauté and wait 30 seconds for the Instant Pot to warm. Pour in the oil and heat for 30 seconds until it starts to sizzle.
2. Add the onion and sauté for 5 minutes, stirring occasionally, until the onion softens. Add the bell pepper and continue to heat, stirring, for another 3 minutes.
3. Mix in the garlic, carrots, crushed tomatoes, fire-roasted tomatoes, soy sauce, and Italian seasoning.
4. Lock the lid into place. Select Pressure Cook and cook on high pressure for 6 minutes. When the cooking is complete, allow the pressure to release naturally for 6 minutes, then quick release any remaining pressure and unlock the lid.
5. Serve warm. If you have any leftovers or are preparing a batch in advance, transfer the sauce to three 16-ounce glass jars or a large (6-cup) glass container and cool before sealing with airtight lid(s). Refrigerate for up to 5 days.

Nutrition Info:
- Per Serving: Calories: 48 ; Fat: 1 g ;Cholesterol: 0 mg ;Sodium: 186 mg

Italian Salad Dressing

Servings: 1
Ingredients:
- 3 tablespoons olive oil
- 2 tablespoons red wine vinegar
- 1 tablespoon freshly squeezed lemon juice
- 2 teaspoons Dijon mustard
- 2 garlic cloves, minced
- 1 teaspoon dried basil
- 1 teaspoon dried parsley
- ¼ teaspoon dried oregano
- ⅛ teaspoon red pepper flakes
- Pinch freshly ground black pepper

Directions:
1. Combine all the ingredients in a jar with a screw cap, cover, and shake to blend. Store in the refrigerator.

Nutrition Info:
- Per Serving: Calories: 48 ; Fat: 3 g ;Cholesterol: 0 mg ;Sodium: 15 mg

Rosemary-Garlic Cashews

Servings: 8
Cooking Time: 10 Minutes
Ingredients:
- 1 tablespoon olive oil
- 2 cups whole cashews
- 1 tablespoon low-sodium soy sauce
- 1 teaspoon garlic powder, divided
- 1 tablespoon chopped fresh rosemary, divided
- 2 teaspoons honey

Directions:
1. Select Sauté and wait 30 seconds for the Instant Pot to warm. Pour in the oil and heat for 30 seconds, until it starts to sizzle. Add the cashews, soy sauce, ½ teaspoon of garlic powder, and 2 teaspoons of rosemary. Cook, stirring, for 3 to 5 minutes, or until the cashews start to brown and their aroma releases.
2. Press Cancel. Mix in the remaining ½ teaspoon of garlic powder, the remaining 1 teaspoon of rosemary, and the honey. Transfer to a parchment paper–lined baking sheet in an even layer, and let cool for 3 minutes before enjoying.

Nutrition Info:
- Per Serving: Calories: 157 ; Fat: 12 g ;Cholesterol: 0 mg ;Sodium: 75 mg

Hot Cocoa Cup

Servings: 2
Cooking Time: 5 Min
Ingredients:
- 1¾ cups vanilla almond milk
- 1 oz 80% dark chocolate, roughly chopped

Directions:

1. Heat the vanilla almond milk in a small stockpot over medium-high heat, and add the chopped chocolate. Once the milk starts to bubble, turn the heat to low.
2. Whisk until the chocolate has melted, and the mixture is fully incorporated. Serve hot.

Nutrition Info:
- Per Serving: Calories: 149 ; Fat: 8 g ;Cholesterol: 0 mg ;Sodium: 105 mg

Chile-Lime Glaze

Ingredients:
- 1 tablespoon avocado oil
- ⅛ teaspoon red pepper flakes
- 2 tablespoons lime juice (about 1 lime)
- 1 teaspoon pure maple syrup

Directions:
1. In a medium mixing bowl, combine the oil, red pepper flakes, lime juice, and maple syrup. Store in an airtight container in the refrigerator for up to 1 week.

Nutrition Info:
- Per Serving: Calories: 48 ; Fat: 5 g ;Cholesterol: 0 mg ;Sodium: 1 mg

Basil-Walnut Pesto

Servings: 1 Cups
Ingredients:
- 2 cups packed basil leaves
- ¼ cup chopped walnuts
- ¼ cup shredded Parmesan cheese
- 3 garlic cloves, peeled
- ½ teaspoon salt
- ¼ cup extra-virgin olive oil

Directions:

1. In a food processor, combine the basil, walnuts, cheese, garlic, and salt. Pulse several times until broken into small pieces.
2. With the food processor running, stream in the oil until smooth.

Nutrition Info:
- Per Serving: Calories: 100 ; Fat: 10 g ;Cholesterol: 0mg ;Sodium: 202 mg

Cherry Chocolate Cake

Servings: 12
Cooking Time: 2 To 2½ Hours
Ingredients:
- Nonstick cooking spray
- 1 cup unsweetened cocoa powder
- 1 cup oat flour, whole-wheat pastry flour, or all-purpose flour
- 1 cup unsweetened dried cherries
- ¼ cup ground flaxseed
- 2 teaspoons baking powder
- ¼ teaspoon salt
- 2 tablespoons extra-virgin olive oil
- 1 large egg
- 2 large egg whites
- 1 tablespoon vanilla extract
- ½ cup granulated sugar
- ½ cup nonfat vanilla Greek yogurt
- ¾ cup low-fat or fat-free milk, or plant-based milk, divided

Directions:
1. Lightly coat the inside of a 6-quart slow cooker with the cooking spray.
2. In a medium bowl, whisk together the cocoa powder, flour, dried cherries, flaxseed, baking powder, and salt.
3. In a separate medium bowl, whisk together the oil, egg, egg whites, and vanilla. Add in the sugar, yogurt, and ¼ cup of milk, mixing thoroughly until no lumps remain. Add the flour mixture and remaining ½ cup of milk, stirring until just combined and incorporated.
4. Spread the batter in the slow cooker. Cover and cook on low for 2 to 2½ hours, or until the center no longer looks moist and feels barely firm to the touch. Remove the lid, turn off the slow cooker, and cool the cake in the ceramic bowl for 15 to 20 minutes before carefully turning it out onto a wire rack to cool completely.
5. Cut into 12 slices and enjoy.

Nutrition Info:
- Per Serving: Calories: 173 ; Fat: 4 g ;Cholesterol: 16 mg ;Sodium: 162 mg

Turkey Stock

Servings: 8
Cooking Time: 8 To 12 Hours
Ingredients:
- Bones, skin, drippings from a roast turkey carcass
- 2 carrots, cut into chunks
- 2 celery ribs, cut into chunks
- 1 onion or leek, chopped
- 2 bay leaves
- 2 or 3 fresh sage or thyme sprigs
- ½ teaspoon salt
- Water to cover, about 10 cups

Directions:
1. Place the turkey bones, skin, and drippings; carrots; celery; onion; bay leaves; sage; and salt in a 6-quart slow cooker. Add the water. Cover and cook on low for 8 to 12 hours.
2. Let the stock cool, then strain it through a fine-mesh strainer, pressing on the solids to release all liquid. Discard the solids.
3. Chill the stock in the refrigerator. As the fat rises to the top and solidifies, you can remove and discard this.
4. Use the stock in your recipes or freeze in 1- or 2-cup portions in airtight containers for up to 3 months.

Nutrition Info:
- Per Serving: Calories: 37 ; Fat: 2 g ;Cholesterol: 7 mg ;Sodium: 196 mg

Whole Wheat Seed Crackers

Servings: 4
Cooking Time: 20 Minutes
Ingredients:
- 1 cup whole wheat flour
- 2 tablespoons ground flaxseed
- 2 tablespoons hemp seeds
- 1 tablespoon za'atar (see Substitution Tip)
- 2 teaspoons garlic powder
- ½ cup water

Directions:
1. Preheat the oven to 400°F. Line a baking sheet with parchment paper.
2. In a large mixing bowl, mix the flour, flaxseed, hemp seeds, za'atar, garlic powder, and water until it is dough-like and slightly sticky.
3. Using a rolling pin or a floured wine bottle, spread the dough to a thickness of about one-tenth of an inch. Cut the dough into bite-size crackers (about 1-by-1-inch) and separate them to allow crispy edges to form on each cracker.
4. Bake for 20 minutes until lightly browned and the edges are crispy. Store in an airtight container for up to 1 week.

Nutrition Info:
- Per Serving: Calories: 163 ; Fat: 5 g ;Cholesterol: 0 mg ;Sodium: 36 mg

Baked Apples With Cranberry-Walnut Filling

Servings: 4
Cooking Time: 7 Minutes
Ingredients:
- 1½ cups water
- 4 medium Honeycrisp or Pink Lady apples
- ⅓ cup walnut pieces
- 2 tablespoons sweetened dried cranberries
- 1 tablespoon brown sugar
- 1 teaspoon ground cinnamon
- 1 tablespoon avocado oil

Directions:

1. Pour 1½ cups of water into the Instant Pot and set the trivet in the center. Core the apples, leaving the bottom intact to form a cup.
2. In a food processor, combine the walnuts and cranberries. Pulse a few times until they form a crumbly consistency. Transfer the mixture to a small bowl. Add the brown sugar, cinnamon, and oil. Mix until well combined.
3. Stuff the apples with equal amounts of the walnut mixture; pack it in well. Place the stuffed apples on the trivet.
4. Lock the lid into place. Select Pressure Cook and cook on high pressure for 7 minutes. When the cooking is complete, allow the pressure to release naturally for 5 minutes, then quick release any remaining pressure and remove the lid.
5. Gently remove each stuffed apple with tongs and serve warm.

Nutrition Info:
- Per Serving: Calories: 194 ; Fat: 8 g ;Cholesterol: 0 mg ;Sodium: 3 mg

Mushroom Gravy

Servings: 2
Cooking Time: 5 To 8 Hours
Ingredients:
- 1 cup button mushrooms, sliced
- ¾ cup low-fat buttermilk
- ⅓ cup water
- 1 medium onion, finely diced
- 2 garlic cloves, minced
- 2 tablespoons extra-virgin olive oil
- 2 tablespoons all-purpose flour
- 1 tablespoon fresh rosemary, minced
- Freshly ground black pepper

Directions:
1. Combine all of the ingredients in a 6-quart slow cooker. Cover and cook on low 5 to 8 hours.
2. Serve warm. Refrigerate leftovers in an airtight container for 3 or 4 days, or freeze for up to 4 months.

Nutrition Info:
- Per Serving: Calories: 54 ; Fat: 4 g ;Cholesterol: 0 mg ;Sodium: 25 mg

Harvest Fruit Crisp

Servings: 6
Cooking Time: 3 Minutes

Ingredients:
- FOR THE CRISP
- 6 small dates, pitted
- 2½ teaspoons avocado oil
- ½ cup gluten-free rolled oats
- 2 tablespoons sliced almonds
- Nonstick cooking spray
- FOR THE FILLING
- 3 medium apples, cored and sliced
- 3 medium pears, cored and sliced
- 2 tablespoons dried cranberries
- 1 tablespoon cornstarch
- 2 teaspoons brown sugar
- Juice of 1 medium lemon

Directions:
1. TO MAKE THE CRISP
2. In a food processor, combine the dates and oil. Process for a minute, then add the oats and pulse just a few times. Remove the blade and scrape down the bowl. Stir in the almonds.
3. Lightly coat the Instant Pot with nonstick spray. Select Sauté and wait 30 seconds for the Instant Pot to warm. Add the crisp mixture and heat for 2 minutes, stirring a few times, until lightly toasted. Press Cancel. Leave the mixture in the pot for 2 minutes more, then transfer to a small bowl.
4. TO MAKE THE FILLING
5. Pour the apples, pears, cranberries, cornstarch, brown sugar, and lemon juice into the Instant Pot and stir well.
6. Lock the lid into place. Select Pressure Cook and cook on high pressure for 3 minutes. When the cooking is complete, allow the pressure to release naturally for 10 minutes, then quick release any remaining pressure and remove the lid.
7. Divide the fruit mixture among six small bowls or ramekins. Top each with about 2 tablespoons of the crisp.

Nutrition Info:
- Per Serving: Calories: 198 ; Fat: 4 g ;Cholesterol: 0 mg ;Sodium: 3 mg

Barbeque Seasoning Rub Blend

Ingredients:
- 2 teaspoons smoked paprika
- 1 teaspoon ground cumin
- ½ teaspoon cayenne pepper
- ½ teaspoon garlic powder
- ½ teaspoon onion powder

Directions:
1. In an empty spice container, mix the paprika, cumin, cayenne pepper, garlic powder, and onion powder until well combined.

Nutrition Info:
- Per Serving: Calories: 1.5 ; Fat:0 g ;Cholesterol: 0 mg ;Sodium: 0.5 mg

Simple Veggie Broth

Servings: 4
Cooking Time: 2 Minutes

Ingredients:
- 2 teaspoons olive oil
- ½ medium red onion, chopped
- 4 cups water
- 1 cup chopped carrots
- 2 medium celery stalks, chopped
- 1 teaspoon garlic powder
- 1 tablespoon Italian seasoning
- 1 tablespoon low-sodium soy sauce
- 1 bay leaf

Directions:
1. Select Sauté and wait 30 seconds for the Instant Pot to warm. Pour in the oil and heat for 30 seconds until it starts to sizzle.
2. Add the onion and cook, stirring occasionally, for 5 minutes, until the onion softens. If the "hot" warning appears, add 1 to 2 tablespoons water.
3. Add the water, carrots, celery, garlic powder, Italian seasoning, soy sauce, and bay leaf.
4. Lock the lid into place. Select Pressure Cook and cook on high pressure for 2 minutes. When the cooking is

complete, allow the pressure to release naturally for 5 minutes, then quick release any remaining pressure and remove the lid.

5. Strain the broth, discard the solids, and use right away, or let cool and then transfer to an airtight container. Refrigerate for up to 4 days or freeze for up to 3 months.

Nutrition Info:
- Per Serving: Calories: 52 ; Fat:0 g ;Cholesterol: 0 mg ;Sodium: 197 mg

Spaghetti Sauce

Servings: ½
Cooking Time: 35 Minutes
Ingredients:
- Olive oil nonstick cooking spray
- ¼ cup chopped onion
- 3 garlic cloves, minced
- 1 (15-ounce) can tomato sauce, no salt added
- ½ cup tomato paste, no salt added
- 1½ cups water
- ½ teaspoon unsweetened cocoa (optional)
- 2 tablespoons dried basil
- 2 teaspoons dried oregano
- ½ teaspoon red pepper flakes
- ⅛ teaspoon salt
- Freshly ground black pepper

Directions:
1. Spray a large skillet with cooking spray and heat over medium heat. Add the onion and garlic to the skillet and sauté for 4 to 5 minutes, or until fragrant and translucent.
2. Add the tomato sauce, tomato paste, and water and stir to combine.
3. Add the cocoa (if using), basil, oregano, red pepper flakes, salt, and a few grinds of pepper and simmer on low for 20 to 30 minutes. Serve over pasta, grains, or vegetables.

Nutrition Info:
- Per Serving: Calories: 36 ; Fat: 0 g ;Cholesterol: 0 mg ;Sodium: 98 mg

Peanut Butter And Chocolate Black Bean Brownie

Servings: 6
Cooking Time: 15 Minutes
Ingredients:
- 1 (15-ounce) can low-sodium black beans, drained and rinsed
- 6 small dates, halved
- 1½ ounces (about half a bar) 70-percent dark chocolate bar, quartered
- 2 tablespoons quick-cooking oats
- 2 tablespoons unsalted raw peanut butter
- 2 tablespoons water

Directions:
1. Preheat the oven to 350°F.
2. In a medium bowl for a food processor, combine the black beans, dates, chocolate, oats, peanut butter, and water. Blend until very smooth and doughy, 2 to 3 minutes.
3. Pour the batter to an 8-inch square baking pan and spread evenly. Cook for about 15 minutes until the top turns a darker brown, is cracked, and a fork comes out clean when inserted in the middle.
4. Let cool for at least 5 minutes before cutting into 6 squares. Store in an airtight container for up to 3 days on the counter.

Nutrition Info:
- Per Serving: Calories: 160 ; Fat: 6 g ;Cholesterol: <1mg ;Sodium: 3 mg

Raspberry-Lime Sorbet

Servings: 2
Ingredients:
- 2 cups frozen raspberries
- 2 teaspoons honey
- 1 teaspoon lime juice
- ½ cup warm water

Directions:
1. In a blender, blend the raspberries, honey, lime juice, and water on high for 2 to 3 minutes until well combined.

2. Place the mixture in a freezer-safe cup or in a ice-pop mold. Freeze 2 to 4 hours until firm. Store in the freezer in an airtight container for up to 1 month.

Nutrition Info:
- Per Serving: Calories: 162 ; Fat: 2 g ;Cholesterol: 0 mg ;Sodium: 10 mg

Garlicky Kale Chips

Servings: 4
Cooking Time: 25 Min
Ingredients:
- 1 bunch curly kale
- 2 teaspoons extra-virgin olive oil
- ¼ teaspoon kosher salt
- ¼ teaspoon garlic powder (optional)

Directions:
1. Preheat the oven to 325°F. Line a rimmed baking sheet with parchment paper.
2. Remove the tough stems from the kale, and tear the leaves into squares about the size of big potato chips (they'll shrink when cooked).
3. Transfer the kale to a large bowl, and drizzle with the oil. Massage with your fingers for 1 to 2 minutes to coat well. Spread out on the baking sheet.
4. Cook for 8 minutes, then toss and cook for another 7 minutes and check them. Take them out as soon as they feel crispy, likely within the next 5 minutes.
5. Sprinkle with salt and garlic powder (if using). Enjoy immediately.

Nutrition Info:
- Per Serving: Calories: 28; Fat: 2 g ;Cholesterol: 0mg ;Sodium: 126mg

Creamy Vegan Alfredo Sauce

Servings: 4
Cooking Time: 7 To 8 Hours
Ingredients:
- 3 cups Savory Vegetable Broth (here) or low-sodium vegetable broth
- 1 cup raw cashews
- 1 cup water
- ½ cup unsweetened soymilk
- ½ cup nutritional yeast
- 1 teaspoon dried mustard
- 2 garlic cloves, minced
- Juice of ½ lemon
- Pinch salt

Directions:
1. Combine all the ingredients in a 6-quart slow cooker and stir well. Cover and cook on low for 7 to 8 hours, until the cashews are softened.
2. Purée the sauce until smooth using an immersion blender.
3. Serve warm.

Nutrition Info:
- Per Serving: Calories: 133 ; Fat: 9 g ;Cholesterol: 0 g ;Sodium: 79 mg

Artichoke-Basil Hummus

Servings: 8
Cooking Time: 15 Minutes
Ingredients:
- 1 (15-ounce) can low-sodium chickpeas, drained and rinsed
- ¼ cup unsalted tahini
- 2 garlic cloves
- 3 tablespoons lemon juice
- 3 tablespoons extra-virgin olive oil
- 1 cup frozen artichoke pieces, defrosted
- 3 tablespoons chopped fresh basil
- 4 tablespoons water
- Freshly ground black pepper

Directions:
1. In a blender, blend the chickpeas, tahini, garlic, lemon juice, olive oil, artichoke, basil, water, and pepper until smooth.

Nutrition Info:
- Per Serving: Calories: 242 ; Fat: 16 g ;Cholesterol: 0 mg ;Sodium: 51 mg

Grano Dolce Light (Sweet Wheat)

Servings: 6
Cooking Time: 30 Min
Ingredients:
- ⅔ cup uncooked farro
- ⅛ teaspoon salt
- ¼ cup walnuts
- ¼ cup almonds
- 1 pomegranate
- 2 tablespoons plus 1 teaspoon honey, divided
- ½ cup 5% plain Greek yogurt
- 1 teaspoon apple cider vinegar
- ¼ teaspoon ground cinnamon
- 2 ounces dark chocolate (70%+ cacao), cut into ½-inch squares

Directions:
1. Preheat the oven to 350°F.
2. Cook the farro with the salt until tender, according to the package directions.
3. Toast the nuts on a rimmed baking sheet in the oven. Shake them after 5 minutes, check after another 3 minutes, and take them out when they look golden and smell nutty, usually after no more than 12 minutes total. Remove from the pan to cool, then chop roughly.
4. Meanwhile, release the pomegranate seeds (see Tip); set them aside.
5. Mix 1 teaspoon of honey into the yogurt in a small bowl.
6. Whisk the vinegar with the remaining 2 tablespoons of honey and the cinnamon in a large bowl. Toss this mixture with the cooked farro.
7. Let it cool to about room temperature, then toss gently with the pomegranate seeds, nuts, and chocolate. Spoon into wine glasses or small mason jars, and top with the sweetened yogurt.

Nutrition Info:
- Per Serving: Calories: 274 ; Fat: 12 g ;Cholesterol: 3 mg ;Sodium: 61 mg

Salt-Free Southwest Seasoning Mix

Servings: ¼ Cup
Cooking Time: 5 Min
Ingredients:
- 2 tablespoons chili powder
- 2 teaspoons garlic powder
- 2 teaspoons onion powder
- 1 teaspoon chipotle powder
- 1 teaspoon dried oregano
- 1 teaspoon dried thyme

Directions:
1. Mix the chili powder, garlic powder, onion powder, chipotle powder, oregano, and thyme together in a small bowl.
2. Store in an airtight container.

Nutrition Info:
- Per Serving: Calories: 11 ; Fat: 0 g ;Cholesterol: 0 mg ;Sodium: 1 mg

Chia Berry Jam

Ingredients:
- 1½ cups frozen mixed berries
- ¼ cup chia seeds
- ½ cup water

Directions:
1. In a medium glass storage container, put the mixed berries, chia seeds, and water. Close the storage container tightly with a secure lid and shake thoroughly. Chill the mixture overnight in the refrigerator.
2. In the morning, using a fork, mix and mash the chia berry mixture to the desired consistency. Store in an airtight container in the refrigerator for up to 5 days.

Nutrition Info:
- Per Serving: Calories: 43 ; Fat: 2 g ;Cholesterol: 0 mg ;Sodium: 3 mg

Spicy Guacamole

Servings: 4
Cooking Time: 15 Min
Ingredients:
- 1 ripe avocado, peeled, pitted, and mashed
- 1½ tablespoons freshly squeezed lime juice
- 1 tablespoon minced jalapeño pepper, or to taste
- 1 tablespoon minced red onion
- 1 tablespoon chopped fresh cilantro
- 1 garlic clove, minced
- ⅛ to ¼ teaspoon kosher salt
- Freshly ground black pepper

Directions:
1. Preheat the oven to 350°F.
2. Brush the oil onto both sides of each tortilla. Stack them on a large cutting board, and cut the entire stack at once, cutting the stack into 8 wedges of each tortilla. Transfer the tortilla pieces to a rimmed baking sheet. Sprinkle a little salt over each chip.
3. Bake for 10 minutes, and then flip the chips. Bake for another 3 to 5 minutes, until they're just starting to brown.

Nutrition Info:
- Per Serving: Calories: 61 ; Fat: 5 g ;Cholesterol: 0mg ;Sodium: 123 mg

Maple Walnuts

Servings: 4
Cooking Time: 2 To 3 Hours
Ingredients:
- 1 pound shelled walnut halves
- ¼ cup maple syrup
- 2 tablespoons extra-virgin olive oil
- ¼ teaspoon ground cinnamon
- 1 teaspoon vanilla extract

Directions:
1. Combine all the ingredients in a slow cooker. Cover and cook on low for 2 to 3 hours, stirring once or twice during cooking to make sure the walnuts remain coated.
2. Spread the nuts across parchment paper to cool.
3. Once completely cooled, store in an airtight container in the refrigerator for 2 to 3 months or in the freezer for up to 6 months.

Nutrition Info:
- Per Serving: Calories: 213 ; Fat: 20 g ;Cholesterol: 0 mg ;Sodium: 0 mg

Lemon-Tahini Dressing

Servings: ¾ Cup
Cooking Time: 5 Min
Ingredients:
- ⅓ cup extra-virgin olive oil
- 2 tablespoons nutritional yeast
- 2 tablespoons freshly squeezed lemon juice
- 2 tablespoons water
- 1 tablespoon reduced-sodium tamari
- 1 tablespoon tahini
- 1 small garlic clove, minced

Directions:
1. Mix the olive oil, nutritional yeast, lemon juice, water, tamari, tahini, and garlic in a mini–food processor, or whisk the ingredients by hand in a large bowl.
2. Store in an airtight container in the refrigerator for up to 1 week.

Nutrition Info:
- Per Serving: Calories: 132 ; Fat: 14 g ;Cholesterol:0 mg ;Sodium: 122 mg

Rosemary And White Bean Dip

Servings: 10
Cooking Time: 10 Min
Ingredients:
- 1 (15-ounce) can cannellini beans, rinsed and drained
- 2 tablespoons extra-virgin olive oil
- 1 garlic clove, peeled
- 1 teaspoon finely chopped fresh rosemary
- Pinch cayenne pepper

- Freshly ground black pepper
- 1 (7.5-ounce) jar marinated artichoke hearts, drained

Directions:
1. Blend the beans, oil, garlic, rosemary, cayenne pepper, and black pepper in a food processor until smooth.
2. Add the artichoke hearts, and pulse until roughly chopped but not puréed.

Nutrition Info:
- Per Serving: Calories: 75 ; Fat: 5 g ;Cholesterol: 0mg ;Sodium: 139mg

Blueberry-Ricotta Swirl

Servings: 2
Cooking Time: 5 Min
Ingredients:
- ½ cup fresh or frozen blueberries
- ½ cup part-skim ricotta cheese
- 1 teaspoon sugar
- ½ teaspoon lemon zest (optional)

Directions:
1. If using frozen blueberries, warm them in a saucepan over medium heat until they are thawed but not hot.
2. Meanwhile, mix the sugar with the ricotta in a medium bowl.
3. Mix the blueberries into the ricotta, leaving a few out. Taste, and add more sugar if desired. Top with the remaining blueberries and lemon zest (if using).

Nutrition Info:
- Per Serving: Calories: 113 ; Fat: 5 g ;Cholesterol: 19 mg ;Sodium: 62 mg

Slow-Cooked Beans

Servings: 6
Cooking Time: 7 To 8 Hours
Ingredients:
- 1 pound dried beans
- Water

Directions:
1. Rinse the beans in a colander and allow to drain.
2. Pour the beans into a 6-quart slow cooker and add enough water to cover beans by 2 inches, about 6 to 8 cups. Let the beans soak for at least 6 hours or overnight. Do not turn the slow cooker on.
3. Rinse and drain the beans again. Return them to the slow cooker and cover with fresh water as in step 2. Cover and cook on low for 7 to 8 hours, or until softened.
4. Drain the beans and let them cool. Freeze them in resealable bags. About 1⅔ cups of cooked beans is the equivalent of a 15-ounce can of beans.

Nutrition Info:
- Per Serving: Calories: 259 ; Fat: 0 g ;Cholesterol: 0 mg ;Sodium: 11 mg

Pumpkin Cakes

Cooking Time: 25 Minutes
Ingredients:
- ¼ cup canned pumpkin purée
- 1 tablespoon unsweetened almond milk or nonfat milk
- 1 tablespoon dark brown sugar
- 1 tablespoon granulated sugar
- 1 tablespoon olive oil
- ½ teaspoon pumpkin pie spice, plus more for garnish
- ¼ cup gluten-free oat flour
- ½ teaspoon baking powder
- ⅛ teaspoon salt

Directions:
1. Preheat the oven to 350°F.
2. In a small bowl, whisk together the pumpkin purée, almond milk, brown sugar, granulated sugar, olive oil, and pumpkin pie spice.
3. Fold in the flour, baking powder, and salt.
4. Divide the mixture evenly between two 4-ounce ramekins and bake for 24 to 26 minutes, or until a toothpick inserted in the center comes out clean.
5. Serve with an extra dusting of pumpkin pie spice.

Nutrition Info:
- Per Serving: Calories: 159 ; Fat: 8 g ;Cholesterol: 0 mg ;Sodium: 155 mg

Mediterranean Seasoning Rub Blend

Ingredients:
- 2 teaspoons garlic powder
- 1½ teaspoon freshly ground black pepper
- 1 teaspoon ground turmeric
- ½ teaspoon smoked paprika
- ½ teaspoon ground cumin

Directions:
1. In an empty spice container, mix the garlic powder, pepper, turmeric, paprika, and cumin until well combined.

Nutrition Info:
- Per Serving: Calories: 2 ; Fat:0 g ;Cholesterol: 0 mg ;Sodium: 0 mg

Date Brownies

Servings: 16
Cooking Time: 30 Minutes
Ingredients:
- Nonstick cooking spray
- 2 cups pitted dates
- 3 large eggs
- 1 cup almond flour
- ½ cup cocoa powder
- ¼ cup avocado oil
- 1 teaspoon baking soda
- Pinch salt

Directions:
1. Preheat the oven to 350°F. Spray an 8-inch baking dish with cooking spray.
2. Bring a small pot of water to a boil over high heat. Remove from the heat.
3. In a bowl, cover the pitted dates with the boiling water, and let soak for 15 minutes. Drain.
4. In a food processor, combine the dates and 2 tablespoons of water. Process until smooth, adding up to 2 tablespoons more water if needed.
5. Add the eggs, one at a time, mixing between each addition.
6. Add the flour, cocoa powder, oil, baking soda, and salt. Mix again. Transfer to the prepared baking dish.
7. Transfer the baking dish to the oven, and bake for 30 minutes, or until a toothpick inserted into the center of the brownies comes out mostly clean. Remove from the oven. Let cool, then cut into 16 pieces.

Nutrition Info:
- Per Serving: Calories: 125 ; Fat: 7 g ;Cholesterol: 0mg ;Sodium: 103 mg

Chocolate Mousse

Servings: 6
Ingredients:
- 1 (3.5-ounce) bar 70-percent dark chocolate
- 1 (14-ounce) package extra-firm tofu, excess water drained and tofu patted dry
- 1 teaspoon pure vanilla extract
- 1 teaspoon honey
- 1 teaspoon cinnamon

Directions:
1. In a medium microwave-safe bowl, heat the chocolate bar in the microwave in 30-second increments until the bar has melted, about 2 minutes.
2. In a blender, blend the tofu, vanilla, honey, cinnamon, and melted chocolate until smooth, about 1 minute, scraping down the sides as needed. Serve as is.
3. The mousse can be stored in an airtight container in the refrigerator for up to 3 days. The mixture may thicken slightly as it cools.

Nutrition Info:
- Per Serving: Calories: 131 ; Fat: 18 g ;Cholesterol: 1 mg ;Sodium: 11 mg

30 Day Meal Plan

Day 1
Breakfast: Multigrain Waffles
Lunch: Southwest Steak Skillet
Dinner: Garbanzo Bean Curry

Day 2
Breakfast: Southwest Breakfast Tofu
Lunch: Grilled Garlic-Lime Chicken
Dinner: Vegan Jambalaya

Day 3
Breakfast: Chocolate Power Smoothie
Lunch: Pineapple Chicken
Dinner: Veggie Pizza With Cannellini Bean Crust

Day 4
Breakfast: Almost-Instant Oatmeal
Lunch: Apple Pork Stir-Fry
Dinner: Vegetarian Gyros

Day 5
Breakfast: Chocolate-Oatmeal Loaf
Lunch: Red Curry Beef Bowls
Dinner: Vegan Chickpea Chili

Day 6
Breakfast: Strawberry Breakfast Sundae
Lunch: Rosemary Lemon Chicken With Vegetables
Dinner: Cauliflower, Tomato, And Green Pea Curry

Day 7
Breakfast: Kidney Bean Tortilla
Lunch: Blueberry, Pistachio, And Parsley Chicken
Dinner: Pantry Beans And Rice

Day 8
Breakfast: Apricot Granola With Fresh Fruit
Lunch: Ras El Hanout Lamb Stew
Dinner: Vegan Red Beans And Rice

Day 9
Breakfast: Sweet Potato And Turkey Hash
Lunch: No-Fuss Turkey Breast
Dinner: Sweet Spot Lentil Salad

Day 10
Breakfast: Shakshuka
Lunch: Balsamic Berry Chicken
Dinner: Cannellini Bean Pizza

Day 11
Breakfast: Eggs In An Avocado
Lunch: Buffalo-Seasoned Chicken Wrap
Dinner: Chickpea And Lentil Ratatouille

Day 12
Breakfast: Peaches And Cream Porridge
Lunch: Tahini And Turmeric Chicken Salad
Dinner: Chickpea And Spinach Saag

Day 13
Breakfast: Lentil Asparagus Omelet
Lunch: Hawaiian Barbeque Chicken
Dinner: White Bean Soup With Orange And Celery

Day 14
Breakfast: Peach-Cranberry Sunrise Muesli
Lunch: Turkey Burgers
Dinner: Spicy Bean And Rice–Stuffed Pepper

Day 15
Breakfast: Cashew Nut Shake
Lunch: Turkey Cauliflower Burgers
Dinner:

Day 16
Breakfast: Tofu Shakshuka

Lunch: Spicy Beef Roast

Dinner: Feta And Black Bean–Stuffed Zucchini

Day 17

Breakfast: Ginger-Mango Smoothie

Lunch: Asian Turkey Lettuce Wraps

Dinner: Chickpea Sloppy Joes

Day 18

Breakfast: Creamy Blueberry Quinoa Porridge

Lunch: Indian Butter Chicken

Dinner: White Bean Cabbage Casserole

Day 19

Breakfast: Strawberry Quinoa

Lunch: Braised Beef

Dinner: Pile-It-High Veggie Sandwich

Day 20

Breakfast: Lemon Ricotta Pancake Bites

Lunch: Mushroom Bolognese

Dinner: Mujaddara

Day 21

Breakfast: Apple Spiced Muffins

Lunch: Chicken Cacciatore

Dinner: Corn, Spinach, And Mushroom Soup

Day 22

Breakfast: Almond Rice Breakfast Pudding

Lunch: Salsa Verde Chicken

Dinner: Butter Bean Penne

Day 23

Breakfast: Breakfast Burrito

Lunch: Beef And Vegetable Stew

Dinner: Spicy Spinach And Almond Stir-Fry

Day 24

Breakfast: Raisin Cashew Oats

Lunch: Sliced Pork Loin For Sandwiches

Dinner: Chickpea Tikka Masala

Day 25

Breakfast: Spinach And Feta Frittata

Lunch: Tomato Chicken Bake

Dinner: Spicy Pear Tacos

Day 26

Breakfast: Potato, Pepper, And Egg Breakfast Casserole

Lunch: Tangy Italian Beef Sandwiches

Dinner: Chickpeas, Tomatoes, And Swiss Chard

Day 27

Breakfast: Kidney Bean Tortilla

Lunch: Lamb Goulash

Dinner: Broccoli And Pasta With Peanut Sauce

Day 28

Breakfast: Shakshuka

Lunch: Spicy Turkey Wraps

Dinner: Pocket Eggs With Sesame Sauce

Day 29

Breakfast: Eggs In An Avocado

Lunch: Parmesan Pork Chops

Dinner: Chickpea Gyros

Day 30

Breakfast: Peaches And Cream Porridge

Lunch: Basil Pesto Chicken

Dinner: Pasta E Fagioli

Recipes Index

A

Acorn Squash Stuffed With White Beans And Kale 77
African Peanut Stew 91
Alberta Steak Salad With Roasted Baby Potatoes 44
Almond Butter And Blueberry Smoothie 17
Almond Rice Breakfast Pudding 28
Almost-Instant Oatmeal 18
Apple Pork Stir-Fry 32
Apple Spiced Muffins 28
Apricot Granola With Fresh Fruit 20
Artichoke, Basil, And Tomato Crustless Quiche 19
Artichoke-Basil Hummus 104
Arugula Salad With Fennel 87
Asian Turkey Lettuce Wraps 38

B

Baby Kale Breakfast Salad With Almond Butter Dressing 24
Baked Apples With Cranberry-Walnut Filling 101
Baked Beet Salad 86
Balsamic Berry Chicken 34
Barbeque Seasoning Rub Blend 102
Basil Pesto Chicken 41
Basil-Walnut Pesto 99
Beef And Vegetable Stew 41
Beet And Fennel Salad 93
Berry, Walnut, And Cinnamon Quinoa Bowl 18
Blueberry, Pistachio, And Parsley Chicken 33
Blueberry-Ricotta Swirl 107
Braised Beef 39
Breakfast Burrito 28
Broccoli And Pasta With Peanut Sauce 76
Broiled Mango 98
Broiled Pesto Cod 50
Brussel Sprouts Hummus 89
Brussels Sprouts And Pancetta 85
Buffalo-Seasoned Chicken Wrap 35
Butter Bean Penne 74
Butternut Soup 82

C

California Scrambled Eggs And Veggies 19
Cannellini Bean Pizza 68
Cashew Nut Shake 24
Cauliflower Steak With Arugula-Basil Pesto 87
Cauliflower, Tomato, And Green Pea Curry 66
Cheesy Kale Chips 97
Cherry Chocolate Cake 100
Chia Berry Jam 105
Chicken Cacciatore 40
Chicken Lettuce Wrap With Peanut Dressing 40
Chickpea And Lentil Ratatouille 68
Chickpea And Spinach Saag 69
Chickpea Gyros 77
Chickpea Sloppy Joes 71
Chickpea Tikka Masala 75
Chickpeas, Tomatoes, And Swiss Chard 76
Chile-Lime Glaze 99
Chocolate And Peanut Butter Smoothie 17
Chocolate Mousse 108
Chocolate Power Smoothie 17
Chocolate-Oatmeal Loaf 18
Cinnamon-Vanilla Custard 96
Citrus Tilapia 48
Cod Parcels With Mushrooms And Spinach 57
Collard Green Halibut Wraps With Cilantro-Mint Sauce 57
Corn, Spinach, And Mushroom Soup 73
Creamy Blueberry Quinoa Porridge 26
Creamy Tuna Salad 56
Creamy Vegan Alfredo Sauce 104
Curried Soup With Cauliflower 79

D

Date Brownies 108

E

Eggs Benedict With Low-Fat Béchamel Sauce 22
Eggs In An Avocado 21
Electric Chickpeas And Shrimp 59

F

Feta And Black Bean–Stuffed Zucchini 70
Fish And Chips With Homemade Tartar Sauce 63
Fish Florentine 48
Flank Steak And Hummus Salad 46
Fruit-Infused Sparkling Water 97

G

Garbanzo Bean Curry 64
Garden Vegetable Stew With Toasted Cashews 92
Garlic-Balsamic Beef Skewers 47
Garlicky Kale Chips 104
Ginger-Mango Smoothie 25
Granny Smith Salad 90
Grano Dolce Light (Sweet Wheat) 105
Greek Yogurt Topped With Turmeric-Spiced Almonds And Pumpkin Seeds 26
Grilled Garlic-Lime Chicken 31

H

Harvest Fruit Crisp 102
Hawaiian Barbeque Chicken 36
Hearty Mashed Potatoes 81
Honey-Glazed Carrots 83
Hot Cocoa Cup 99

I

Indian Butter Chicken 38
Italian Salad Dressing 98

K

Kefir Parfait With Chia Berry Jam 22
Kidney Bean Tortilla 20

L

Lamb Goulash 45
Lemon & Lime Tuna 49
Lemon Chicken Orzo Soup 88
Lemon Ricotta Pancake Bites 27
Lemon-Basil Chicken With Baby Bell Peppers 43
Lemon-Roasted Asparagus 88
Lemon-Rosemary Salmon 55
Lemon-Tahini Dressing 106
Lentil And Fennel Salad 79
Lentil Asparagus Omelet 23
Lentil, Raisin, And Pecan Stuffed Acorn Squash 64
Lentil-Walnut Bolognese 78
Lime Wild Rice 81

M

Mahi Mahi With Leeks, Ginger, And Baby Bok Choy 53
Maple Walnuts 106
Mediterranean Cucumber, Tomato, And Kalamata Olive Salad 83
Mediterranean Mahi-Mahi 54
Mediterranean Seasoning Rub Blend 108
Middle Eastern Bulgur Pilaf 82
Minestrone Soup 89
Mixed Veg Crisps 95
Moroccan Spiced Red Lentil And Millet Stew 93
Mujaddara 72
Multigrain Waffles 16
Mushroom And Thyme Gravy 96
Mushroom Bolognese 39
Mushroom Gravy 101
Mushroom, Zucchini, And Chickpea Stuffed Tomatoes 71
Mussels With White Wine Sauce 55
Mustard-Dill Salmon With Lemon And Asparagus 52

N

No-Fuss Turkey Breast 34

O

Oat Risotto With Mushrooms, Kale, And Chicken 44
Omelet With Zucchini, Mushrooms, And Peppers 26
One-Skillet Southwest Quinoa And Vegetables 69
Open-Faced Lemon Pepper Tuna Melt 62
Orange And Avocado Green Salad 82

P

Pan-Seared Halibut With Chimichurri 56
Pan-Seared Pork Medallions With Pears 43
Pan-Seared Salmon With Chimichurri Sauce 53
Pantry Beans And Rice 66
Parmesan Pork Chops 42
Pasta E Fagioli 78
Peach-Cranberry Sunrise Muesli 23
Peaches And Cream Porridge 22
Peanut Butter And Chocolate Black Bean Brownie 103
Pile-It-High Veggie Sandwich 72
Pine Nut Haddock 48
Pineapple Chicken 32
Pistachio Flounder Fillets 50
Pistachio-Crusted Halibut 51
Poached Fish In Tomato-Caper Sauce 49
Pocket Eggs With Sesame Sauce 77
Polenta Cakes 91
Potato, Pepper, And Egg Breakfast Casserole 29
Pumpkin Cakes 107

Q

Quick Kale Caesar Salad 87
Quinoa Spinach Power Salad 86
Quinoa, Pistachio, And Blueberry Breakfast Bowl 25

R

Rainbow Trout Fillets With Parsley, Pecan, And Oranges 51
Raisin Cashew Oats 29
Ras El Hanout Lamb Stew 34
Raspberry-Lime Sorbet 103
Red Beans, Sausage, And Rice 38
Red Curry Beef Bowls 32
Roasted Eggplant With Tahini-Garlic Dressing 93
Roasted Lentil Snack Mix 85
Roasted Peppers And Zucchini 90
Roasted Summer Squash Farro Salad 94
Roasted Sweet Potatoes 84
Root Vegetable Stew 85
Rosemary And White Bean Dip 106
Rosemary Lemon Chicken With Vegetables 33
Rosemary Sweetato Mash 84
Rosemary-Garlic Cashews 99
Rosemary-Lemon Salmon 61

S

Sage-Roasted Baby Carrots 90
Salmon Burgers With Dill 60
Salmon En Papillote With Sugar Snap Peas, Tomatoes, And Thyme 60
Salmon Over Lentils 52
Salmon Sage Bake 61
Salsa Verde Chicken 40
Salt-Free Southwest Seasoning Mix 105
Sardines Puttanesca 58
Sautéed Kale With Blood Orange Dressing 81
Sesame-Garlic Edamame 97
Shakshuka 21
Sheet Pan Tahini Cod With Broccoli 57
Shrimp Paella 54
Shrimp Scampi 58
Simple Roasted Peppers 94
Simple Veggie Broth 102
Sliced Pork Loin For Sandwiches 46
Slow-Cooked Beans 107
Sofrito Cod Stew 52
Soft-Boiled Egg Bites With Apricot Cheese Toasts 30
Southwest Breakfast Tofu 16
Southwest Steak Skillet 31
Southwest Sweet Potato Breakfast Hash 24
Spaghetti Sauce 103
Spaghetti Squash Stuffed With Kale, Artichokes, And Chickpeas 75
Spicy Bean And Rice–Stuffed Peppers 70
Spicy Bean Soup 84
Spicy Beef Roast 37
Spicy Guacamole 106
Spicy Herring Pasta 50
Spicy Pear Tacos 75
Spicy Spinach And Almond Stir-Fry 74
Spicy Turkey Wraps 42
Spinach And Feta Frittata 29
Strawberry Breakfast Sundae 19

Strawberry Quinoa 27

Sweet Potato And Turkey Hash 21

Sweet Spot Lentil Salad 68

Swiss Chard And Tzatziki Dip On Whole Wheat Toast 17

T

Tahini And Black Bean–Stuffed Sweet Potatoes 67

Tahini And Turmeric Chicken Salad 36

Tangy Italian Beef Sandwiches 45

Tempeh Taco Salad With Chile-Lime Glaze 91

Tofu And Veggie "Ramen" With Soba Noodles 73

Tofu Shakshuka 25

Tomato And Zucchini With Salmon And Farro 54

Tomato Chicken Bake 45

Tuna, Cashew, And Couscous Salad 56

Turkey And Mushroom Wild Rice Casserole 41

Turkey Burgers 36

Turkey Cauliflower Burgers 37

Turkey Stock 100

Tuscan Turkey, White Beans, And Asparagus 35

U

Umami Mushrooms 86

V

Vanilla Pear Crisp 96

Vegan Chickpea Chili 66

Vegan Jambalaya 64

Vegan Red Beans And Rice 67

Vegetable Chips With Rosemary Salt 88

Vegetable Curry 80

Vegetarian Gyros 65

Veggie Pizza With Cannellini Bean Crust 65

W

Walnut-And-Herb–Crusted Fish 58

Walnut-Crusted Halibut 60

Warm Balsamic Beet Salad With Sunflower Seeds 92

Weeknight Fish Skillet 59

White Bean Cabbage Casserole 72

White Bean Soup With Orange And Celery 69

Whole Wheat Seed Crackers 101

Z

Za'Atar Cod Fillets 59

Zesty Carrot Tomato Sauce 98

Zucchini Noodles 89

Printed in Great Britain
by Amazon